FINDING THE WORK THAT'S RIGHT FOR YOU

The Great Niche Hunt

David J. Frähm
with Paula Rinehart

NAVPRESS®
A MINISTRY OF THE NAVIGATORS
P.O. BOX 6000, COLORADO SPRINGS, COLORADO 80934

The Navigators is an international Christian
organization. Jesus Christ gave His followers
the Great Commission to go and make disciples
(Matthew 28:19). The aim of The Navigators is
to help fulfill that commission by multiplying
laborers for Christ in every nation.

NavPress is the publishing ministry of The
Navigators. NavPress publications are tools
to help Christians grow. Although publications alone cannot make disciples or change
lives, they can help believers learn biblical
discipleship, and apply what they learn to their
lives and ministries.

Library of Congress Catalog Card Number:
    90-63220
ISBN 08910-96116

Cover illustration: Bob Fuller
Interior illustrations: Anne E. Frähm

The following terms used in this book are
trademarks: "The Great Niche Hunt"; "Whole
Life Resume"; "Functional Design."

Printed in the United States of America

CONTENTS

To
the memory of Bryan Dixon,
whose death helped awaken me
to the realities of my life,

my wife, Anne Elizabeth Frähm,
whose battle with cancer
has helped me learn how to live my life,

my dad, Paul Frähm,
who has always allowed me
to choose my own path in life,

my friend and mentor, Stacy Rinehart,
who encouraged me to "polish and publish"
what I had to say about life,

my kids, Jessica and Ben,
who have allowed me to celebrate
the individual uniquenesses of life.

AUTHORS

David J. Frähm was born and lived most of his years up through college in Iowa. It was while attending the University of Iowa in the early 1970s that he came into contact with The Navigators, and in 1977 he joined their staff.

His double degrees from the University of Iowa in psychology and anthropology fueled his intense interest in understanding the patterns and uniquenesses of both the individual and his or her cultural context.

David has served in several capacities with The Navigators, including Director of campus ministry at the University of Wisconsin-LaCrosse; Associate Director of the Navigators' Leadership Development Institute in Colorado Springs; and Personnel Director of the Glen Eyrie Conference Center. He currently serves as Career Consultant and Assessment Specialist within the Navigator organization.

David and his wife, Anne, live in Colorado Springs. They have two children: Jessica and Benjamin.

Paula Corn Rinehart is a graduate of the University of Tennessee, where she was involved with the Navigator ministry. She has been an editor for NavPress.

Paula and her husband, Stacy, are the authors of *Choices: Finding God's Way in Dating, Sex, Singleness, and Marriage* (NavPress, 1982). She is also the author of Bible studies for preteens—*Stuck Like Glue, One of a Kind,* and *Never Too Small for God* (NavPress, 1989).

Paula and Stacy have two children: Allison and Brady.

ACKNOWLEDGMENTS

I owe a great deal of thanks to those who have gone before me in the fields of individual assessment and career pathing: Bernard Haldane and his *Success Factor Analysis* (SFA); Ralph Mattson and Arthur Miller and their *System for Identifying Motivated Abilities* (SIMA); Richard Bolles and his ever-present influence on the field through his ever-expanding masterpiece entitled *What Color Is Your Parachute?*; Isabel Briggs Myers, who even at the ripe old age of eighty-two was at work revising and improving upon her *Myers-Briggs Type Indicator* (MBTI) before death overtook her. Through their books and their ideas, these individuals, among others, have been my mentors and my heroes.

Then, too, I must give a one-man standing ovation to my editorial sidekick, Paula Rinehart. "Writing a book," she once observed, "is like trying to wrestle a snake into a pop bottle."

Now that I've finished this process I understand what she meant. Indeed, it has not been easy. My job was to have the ideas and put them into words—hers was to take my words and bring them to life. She has a wonderful gift from God of weaving language into living color. I am thankful for her work with me on this project.

I must also acknowledge the many people whose stories I have told or drawn from in this book. I consider the facts and stories of a person's life hidden treasure waiting to be discovered and valued. A big thanks to those folks who have allowed me to mine the treasure in their lives.

INTRODUCTION

There are many, many books on the market that deal with the career pathing process and its numerous facets. Being a collector is part of the way God has put me together, and as such, I've amassed many of these books on the shelves in my office. The complexity of some of these documents can be overwhelming, especially for an individual like myself who enjoys simplifying and summarizing. If you've been involved in your own "niche hunt" for very long, perhaps you too have been overwhelmed.

My intention in writing this book is to be simple, pointed, relevant—and to address my subject matter with the wisdom earned within the boundaries of my own life experiences. What I have not lived, I have not written. What I have written speaks most knowingly to individuals feeling their way through mid-life transition—that period between the ages of thirty-something and fifty-something when the questions, "Who am I?" and "What do I really want to accomplish with my life?" become most poignant.

At the time of my writing, the primary audience going through this mid-life transition is that huge group of people known to American society as the "Baby Boom" genera-tion--76 million of us born between 1946 and 1964. It'll be the year 2014 before the last of the official "Boomers" turns fifty.

And what then of the next generation, the one in which my kids are growing up? By the year 2014 they will be thirty-five and thirty-two. How will they deal with the issues of life and work in this world—the world that God has created and their parents have helped to shape? Will they need the same input and ideas that are contained in this book for today? I think so. American society will never outgrow its need to revere God, to identify and celebrate the uniqueness of the individual created in His image, and to practice biblical stew-ardship in vocational choices.

This is a book about work and finding your place in it—but even more, it is a book about life. I hope that the thoughts you find in it will not only help facilitate your search for suitable employment, but will also help you to develop a "philosophy of life"—a biblical stewardship of self—to be lived out as a testimony to your Creator within the spheres of your work and influence in His world.

I'm an Iowan at heart. I may live in the stratospheres of Colorado, but my mindset is definitely "earthy." I tire quickly of reading—much less writing—lofty platitudes concerning the Christian experience that seem distant and unrelated to our every day existence. I want what I write to be real and not decaffeinated; served up hot and black, without sugar. For that reason, my style of writing involves telling a great many stories of real-life situations. I hope you enjoy my nitty-gritty approach.

After you've read and digested the contents of this book, I'd dearly love to hear from you. Send me a letter with your thoughts, your dreams, your feedback, your questions, your disappointments, your successes. As I said, I'm a collector. I guarantee that I'll read your letters and save them—perhaps as content for a future book—and will try to respond to you as soon as possible.

You can get in touch with me at the following address:

David J. Frähm
c/o The Navigators
P.O. Box 6000
Colorado Springs, CO 80934

CHAPTER ONE

WHEN FEELING BAD ABOUT WORK IS GOOD
The Need to Find the Right Job Fit

If you're in the wrong place, the right place is empty!

Original author unknown

As soon as I heard Robert's voice on the phone, I could tell he was shaken. Something was wrong. *Very* wrong.

"Get over here as quickly as you can," he said. "Bryan's been hurt."

I grabbed Bryan's brother Kevin and a few of the guys who were helping me clean the windows of the large three-story house we were renting for the summer. We piled in the car and raced the half mile to the site where Bryan and his friends had spent this Saturday morning painting. A small crowd of college students had gathered on the pavement outside.

In the center of that crowd lay Bryan—unconscious, deathly pale, and limp as a rag doll. He had obviously taken a terrible fall. A short, slender woman was bent over his broken form, forcing her air into his lungs as she struggled to keep torn fragments of his head in place.

15

In the distance I could now hear the ambulance siren coming closer, its lone wail piercing the still Minnesotan morning. I didn't know then how badly Bryan was hurt, but I knew the picture before me wasn't a hopeful one.

Bryan Dixon was a college student at the University of Wisconsin-LaCrosse whom I had recruited to a summer training program for Christians that summer in Minneapolis. His brother and I were part of a similar program down the street. During the daytime we worked at whatever jobs we could find around campus. That left our nights free for study and fun and talking with other students about Christ. In all our summers of working and studying together, no one had ever been hurt. That's part of what made Bryan's accident so hard.

I pieced together the story. Bryan and Mitch had been perched at the top of thirty-foot ladders as they painted the trim of the old sorority house. One minute they were discussing their plans for when school started again. The next minute Bryan turned strangely quiet. His paintbrush fell out of his hand. His eyes closed. And as if it were a movie in slow motion, Mitch watched Bryan's frame go limp and tumble off the ladder. With nothing to break the fall, he landed head first on the pavement thirty feet below.

After Bryan was rushed to the hospital, we began a vigil by his side with his family, praying that he would wake up. It seemed he should just open his eyes, take the needles from his arms and legs, get up and walk out of that hospital room.

But Bryan didn't get up. I found myself staring at his still form on the white sheets with tubes coming in and out of everywhere, and I struggled to recall the real Bryan—the eager, athletic guy I had gotten to know over coffee in the student union that year.

Bryan was the kind of person you just immediately liked. Even though he was only twenty-one, he seemed to know exactly where he was heading in life. He had been full of dreams and plans for combining Spanish and a love of computers to make a difference in his world for God. He was a kid with convictions. I liked that. Over the year we had gotten to be good friends.

Bryan's lifeless body in that hospital bed was a silent reminder of how easily our dreams and plans can come crashing down—of how short life really is.

Over the next four days, doctors performed a series of operations to relieve the pressure and fluid in Bryan's brain. But with each passing day, there was less and less hope that Bryan would recover. On the same day that Bryan's friends finished their program and left for home, he was pronounced officially dead. His parents buried him in the cemetery across the street from the university dormitory in LaCrosse, Wisconsin, where he'd spent so many hours preparing for a life he wasn't going to live.

In a few short weeks another fall semester would begin. Another round of football games, classwork, and ministry activities. Another set of students looking for some answers to life and work and relationships and God. I was the campus director for this collegiate ministry—but I was now too numb to rise to the challenge.

Everyone has turning points: some event or experience that is an inner watershed, a before-and-after happening. Bryan's death was that turning point for me.

Suddenly, it seemed, the time was now to figure out whether the direction I was heading in life was really the one I ought to take. I was thirty-two years old, married with two children, and for five years now I had been pioneering a campus ministry for college students. I started to wonder—was this *really* what I wanted to do with my work life—those sixty hours a week that turn into months and years and add up to a lifetime spent in some particular direction?

Was I following God's vocational guidance for me, or had I slipped into conforming to the patterns and expectations of others—like a circus dog jumping through all the right hoops? Although my roles were clear, my reasons for performing them no longer were. In my more honest moments, I had to admit I enjoyed less and less this job of organizing and motivating college students—a worthwhile task to be sure, but I questioned just how gifted I was to do it. I realized I was just going through the motions.

What was it that I really wanted to gain from and contribute to my world over the long haul . . . or whatever haul I had left? What kinds of plans did God have for me—not me the generic person, but *me,* the unique individual?

These questions and the subsequent months of study were a kind of mental and spiritual wandering for me, a time of groping for answers to the mystery of who I was and where I fit, especially in the world of work.

THE COMMON QUESTION

In the years since that watershed experience, I've realized how many others harbor serious questions about how they ought to spend their days. Adam's original task was clear: tend the garden for God. But the rest of us seem to wander over less clearly marked terrain, with a confusing array of options that define our word *work.* We struggle to find the niche where we belong. We ask that most basic of questions: *Where do I fit?*

Not long ago my wife and I sat in the living room of a friend's home sharing coffee and conversation with a collection of friends we call a fellowship group. That night the conversation turned to the issue of work. The host posed an intriguing question: "What would you be doing with your life if time and money were no issue?" I sat back to listen.

As the question drifted around the room, individuals responded by picturing a future career scenario as best they could. I couldn't help noticing that except for my wife and me and one other man, all of them indicated that their current vocational choice was not enough to keep them motivated if time and money were no issue. Many had only a vague idea of what they wanted to be doing—they just knew that what they *were* doing wasn't it!

Elizabeth, a tall, attractive woman in her early thirties,

has been selling insurance for several years. She was the first to respond. "In college I did the practical thing. I took some courses in theater, but then I opted out for a degree in economics." Only now has Elizabeth started to admit to herself that working with accounts and sales figures every day is something she deeply dislikes—something that leaves her bank account full but her creativity untouched. She said she feels like she's been on a treadmill where her goal is to meet the requirements or expectations that others have for her. Now she's tired of doing the predictable, practical thing.

What Elizabeth said struck a chord with others. How many of us, I wonder, chose a career direction in which we are spending a sizable portion of our life because some significant person implied that being an elementary school teacher or a baseball coach or a mechanical engineer would be the right occupation for us? And now we discover that we are mismatched for the job we're doing.

A lanky, easygoing guy named Jim began to talk. He was just graduating from college. "My dilemma is this," he confessed. "I've got my life all planned out—but without any consideration for what I'd really like to do or what I'd be good at, or even what God would want. I feel like I've been on an academic merry-go-round and I want to get off, but I don't know where to jump." Jim's engineering course work is more a reflection of his high SAT math scores than of any particular interest or bent in that direction. Now he's about to graduate—to be launched in a direction he's not sure he wants to go.

That night I was reminded of a recent study indicating that the number of Americans who are mismatched with their work may be as high as eighty percent.

From my experience in helping people find their niche in the world of work, I would say that figure is accurate. And the reason there are so many of us dissatisfied with our jobs is that, like Jim, we survey the possible job scene with little accurate knowledge of who we are as individuals and a great deal of indecision about what we really want to accomplish in life through our work. Then, once we're entrenched, the job becomes a matter of survival rather than satisfaction.

One other person's comments from our group discussion that night were particularly relevant to these issues. They illustrate the subtle distinctions we make to decide, as Christians, which work matters most—to God and, therefore, to us.

Scott works for a Christian organization. Many would assume he's found the perfect spot—working "directly for God." The only problem is that as Scott sits at his desk each day preparing for the people he will see, he dreams of farming—raising pigs! He is plagued by questions: "Am I just being selfish?" he wondered aloud. "Am I overlooking the great needs of the city? Will people think I'm quitting or deserting them if I go back to hog farming?"

I could tell that Scott felt trapped. He knew what he'd *like* to be doing, but he questioned its value to God. So did some of his well-meaning friends.

FINDING YOUR NICHE

The way many people feel about the jobs they do makes for catchy bumper stickers. "Work is a four-letter word," proclaims one. "Help, I'm a POW . . . Prisoner of Work," reads another. And then my favorite: "I owe, I owe, it's off to work I go." Evidently, for too many of us, work is just something we grind out for a paycheck that covers the interest on our credit cards! I think—in fact I *know*—that work can be more than that.

You know how off-balance it looks when a tall man dances with a tiny woman. You understand a toddler's frustration as she tries to force the proverbial square peg into a round hole. Well, that's exactly what happens to many of us every day, nine to five, in our jobs. We are disappointed in the world of work because we are spending so many hours trying to squeeze ourselves into a job that just isn't the right size or shape.

In their book *Finding a Job You Can Love*, Ralph Mattson and Arthur Miller (leading authorities in issues of individual design and job fit) present their findings from a number of professions they've surveyed. They note that two-thirds of those in the teaching profession aren't motivated to teach. They're simply wired together as individuals to do something else besides dispense information to waiting students eight hours a day. The authors' interviews with managers and executives revealed the same: only one out of three was well matched to the job.[1]

The gaps in the process that allow such a mismatch start early. Few of us get off to the right start vocationally. In her book *The Postponed Generation*, Susan Littwin notes a national survey of over a quarter million 1982 college freshmen that showed only 5.6 percent had any intention of seeking help in determining their vocation.[2] At the end of their college careers they show up on the doorstep of a placement office, desperate. "The majority of college seniors we see are not sure what they want to do," says Lisa Heiser, a career development specialist at the University of Minnesota. "They tell us they're open to absolutely anything because they need a job."[3]

"I need a job." That sounds familiar, doesn't it? And that's true—you *do* need a job. But eventually, the only kind of job you're going to be satisfied with—and be really good at—is a job that fits the way God has *designed* you to function and in some fundamental way satisfies the *desires* for contribution that He has planted in your head and cultivated in your heart.

The real danger is that we'll adopt a work-is-a-necessary-evil attitude. One woman who attended my "Niche Hunt" classes repeated her mother's advice, which epitomizes the idea that life begins on Friday afternoon and ends on Sunday night. She told her daughter: "Don't worry too much about finding work that fits you and that you really enjoy. I've been through all that before. It's a phase—a lot like the beginning of marriage. First, you think it's going to be great. You're all excited. But then you just get used to it. Pretty soon, you're just putting up with the whole thing."

That attitude of "just putting up with a job" eventually leads to a day of reckoning—more popularly known as a "mid-life crisis." You start to feel as though you're missing out on something you can't quite name. "I fell in step in my job rather mindlessly—just trying to do what my company wanted," a friend confided recently. "Now I'm trying to figure out who I am and what I really want to give to my world through my work."

Indeed, these are the two questions that I want to help you ask and answer:

- Who am I?
- What do I really want to give to my world through my work?

There are about forty million of us who are now negotiating this mid-life passage—and with it, all the questions of whether we're really doing what we ought and want to be doing, since if we aren't, the time to figure that out is now. The fact that we have been herded together in the much-heralded, much-lamented Baby Boom generation since infancy has only made us more anxious to understand our unique contribution *as individuals.* We tire more easily of managing another person's vision or goals. Possessing a strong sense of the stewardship of our work lives, the question of discerning where we fit becomes critical for each of us.

Sometimes, only a crisis will move us forward in the discovery process. For me, Bryan's death was just such a wake-up call. It caused me to pay serious attention for the first time in my life to clearly identifying the design God had given me for optimum functioning in His world. With the same seriousness I began clarifying the desires and dreams God had planted in me concerning what I wanted to give to

His world. The process of self-discovery and career redirection I went through forms the basis of this book.

Granted, some people are in situations in life in which simple survival is a daily struggle. To address my thoughts about job fit toward them would be irrelevant, if not blatantly offensive. This book is for people with choices. If you're living above the "survival mode," you probably have more choices than you've recognized or have let yourself believe. And with more choices comes more responsibility.

It's a tragedy when individuals—especially Christians—who have a variety of choices and options allow themselves to be trapped, for whatever reasons, within realms of work for which they are unmotivated. Imagine investing eight hours a day, five days a week, fifty weeks a year—*eighty thousand hours* over a working life span of forty years or so—all in work that you don't care for or that doesn't fit you. That's a waste of life! And it's not good advertising for the Originator of the whole idea of work, either.

What I'm talking about is a lack of stewardship—the stewardship of being who God made you to be and accomplishing what He's put on your heart to accomplish. Whoever you are, whatever you are—you are a valuable, unique individual. It's important that you discover your own *vocational stewardship,* that place of vocational functioning in God's world of work in which your design comes together with your desires to form a motivated platform from which to represent the values of your Creator.

Chapter 2 of this book celebrates the value of all work done in God's name. Chapter 3 celebrates the uniqueness of you the individual, created in His image. Chapters 4 through 7 will help you discover the elements of your design, the ways you prefer to operate. And finally, the goal of chapters 8 and 9 is to help you clarify your vocational vision: what you want to give to your world through your work.

When Elizabeth Dole delivered her acceptance speech for the post of Secretary of Labor in the Bush administration, one thing she said was that she wanted to "move beyond full employment to fulfilling employment."[4]

I hope to do for you in this book what possibly Elizabeth Dole cannot. I want to help you as a unique individual discover your niche in the world of work.

CHAPTER TWO

PRIESTS IN WORK CLOTHES
Did God Really Mean for Work to Be a Four-Letter Word?

The fact is that creation and cultivation, nature and culture, raw materials and craftsmanship belong together. As Luther put it, "God even milks the cow through you." This concept of divine-human collaboration applies to all honorable work. God has so ordered life on earth as to depend on us.

John R. W. Stott[1]

I once read a fascinating book written by an old man near the end of his life. He had made a lifelong project of studying people and what fulfilled them. A vast inheritance from his father had made possible this search, and unlike you or me his bottomless checking account meant that he could pursue whatever he fancied. So what I had before me to read was simply the cream of all he had learned.

Early in his life, it seems, this man immersed himself in the academic world, thinking that perhaps education and intellect could unlock the mysteries of a fulfilling life. He was a brilliant man who easily outstripped his peers in the pursuit of knowledge. But all his knowledge only left him more aware of the grief and pain that etches so much of life.

Alternatively, perhaps fulfillment could be found in the party scene, he reasoned. So he decided to live his life with no other purpose in mind than pleasure. But this, too, was a dead end. *Could it be,* he thought to himself, *that in the final analysis, life is something of a melancholy joke best numbed by alcohol or a big laugh?*

Before long, though, the man tired of such emptiness and turned his attention toward more pragmatic projects. He built beautiful homes for himself with spacious parks and gardens. An army of servants watched over his estate, especially his herd of prize horses. Now, having built and bought and acquired every comfort imaginable, he started to collect women as well. Whatever and whomever he desired was his to enjoy.

Then came what I thought was the most intriguing part of this man's story. Only after he had it all did he realize what he really lacked. He returned to the God of his youth with the conviction that a life that excluded God was not much of a life at all.

"When all is said and done," he concluded, "fear God and keep His commandments."

By now you've probably recognized this man as the famous writer of Ecclesiastes, King Solomon. I like to rephrase Solomon's conclusions like this:

> Our life and work in the world and our pursuit of
> fulfillment is, in the final analysis, self-centered,
> meaningless, and empty without God. But when we
> turn to Him, when we make the fundamental deci-
> sion to center our existence in a relationship with our
> Creator—then and only then does our life take on pur-
> pose and our work have the potential to bring joy and
> satisfaction.

Learn this clear lesson from Solomon's life: *Fulfillment in your work begins with a vital relationship with your Creator.* Without this essential foundation you would, no doubt, still find work to occupy your waking hours. But in the end, I think you would know only the empty regrets of a life half lived. Only the person who is deeply related to God has the potential of fulfilling Thoreau's dream: to live "deliberately," so that when it comes time to die you don't feel you have never really lived at all.

The first step in your own great niche hunt must be this: *Make it your purpose to be God's person in His world.*

WORK AS GOD'S SELF-EXPRESSION

"In the beginning God created the heavens and the earth" (Genesis 1:1). It would be difficult to find any more celebrated sentence in the Bible than this. Astronauts quote it, scientists debate it; but how this declaration relates to your work life is my concern here. The fact that God begins His communication to us with a picture of Himself "at work" should intersect with our outlook on the hours we spend in a job.

That opening line teaches us that all that exists, including you and me, is here because there is a God who has expressed Himself in His work.

The Bible devotes its opening chapters to telling the story of God's work, His creativity—His self-expression. To see work in this light, I believe, is to see work as God intended it. God is a worker, and in His work He tells us of Himself. It is as though He says to us, "Do you want to know something of the essence of who I am, of My character? Then watch Me work."

The heavens declare the glory of God;
    the skies proclaim the work of his hands.
Day after day they pour forth speech;
    Night after night they display knowledge.
There is no speech or language
    where their voice is not heard.
Their voice goes out into all the earth,
    their words to the ends of the world.
(Psalm 19:1-4)

Work is God's self-expression—yet He has designed us to participate in it with Him. His image in us insists on being expressed through our work—our own self-expression. "The Creator," says theologian John Stott, "has deliberately humbled Himself to require the cooperation of human beings. He created the earth, but entrusted to humans the task of subduing it. He planted a garden, but then appointed a gardener."[2] Our work is to be a participation with God in expressing His image in His world.

Nowhere else in Scripture is this better seen than in Genesis 2:19-20—

> Now the LORD God had formed out of the ground all the beasts of the field and all the birds of the air. He brought them to the man to see what he would name them; and whatever the man called each living creature, that was its name. So the man gave names to all the livestock, the birds of the air and all the beasts of the field.

What a fascinating picture of the colaborship between God and man! God created the animals; Adam gave them names. Imagine the creative juices that must have been coursing through Adam's veins. That God allows the people He creates such responsibility and freedom is amazing. In some mysterious way, God has arranged life on earth to be dependent upon *our* contribution.

From this perspective, work is much more than a necessary evil to pay the bills or maintain a certain lifestyle. It's an opportunity to labor with God in His creation—to exalt Him by expressing His image in the world. Our work ought to be a reflection of God's character.

God has made each of us His representative steward, assigned to some tailored role in "tending His garden." We know that God has the whole world in His hands, certainly—but the question to ask is, What part of it has He assigned to your care?

JUST WHAT ON EARTH IS GOD'S WORK?

In the beginning, God created everything. Most of us know the creation story almost by heart. But bear with me while I go back to it, because I want to illustrate my growing conviction that the story we *tell* is not the story we really *believe*. Here's the version I think most of us unwittingly subscribe to:

> In the beginning, the earth was a nondescript kind of place—dark, empty, undefined. But not for long, because God was there and He was making a masterpiece.
>
> His first step was to shine some light on all this darkness. "Let there be light," He said. Sure enough, there was light. He separated the light from the darkness and called the light "day" and the darkness "night."
>
> He sorted the sky from the earth and the sea from the land. In that mode He continued all week long, creating and separating, sorting and dividing.
>
> Then Saturday came—and with it, His truly crowning achievement. God made a man. He designed two different models, a "male" man and a "female" man.
>
> By then, it was Sunday morning. God took the day off.
>
> But early Monday morning, He woke up with a jolt. His "male" man and "female" man were going to need something to do. So God created the idea of work. And He saw that the idea was good.
>
> But God saw that not all work was equally good. So God separated work into two kinds. The good work He called "sacred," and the less-good work He called "secular."
>
> And from that day forward, God has been able to tell who really loves Him the most by whether they decide to do the good work or the less-good work.

The story sounds a bit preposterous this way, doesn't it? But I think this is the edition many of us believe. Somewhere along the line, we took the "separation" theme evident in creation and attached it to the job description God gave to humans. Some work became known as "God's work," while other work was called secular. And there the problems began.

My own story is a case in point. In the early '70s when I was a student at the University of Iowa, our Christian group used to have the rallying call, "Sell the farm." To us it meant that nothing else in all of life should distract us from serving Jesus. "Sell the farm" was our way of encouraging each other to keep our focus on the authority of Christ. Unfortunately, the phrase began to take on a meaning all its own, with a mandate it was never intended to endorse.

The upper Midwest is not only part of the famous Bible Belt, it's also home to some of the finest dirt in the world. Agriculture is its heartbeat. Farming was a prominent vocational pursuit among the college students who were coming to Christ at the university. Many of them were planning agricultural careers after graduation.

You can probably already guess at what started to happen. Anyone who thinks deeply about what it means to follow Jesus wrestles with the question of whether his contemplated career will be a spiritual detour or opportunity. For our would-be farmers, the slogan that was intended to emphasize the value of Christ's preeminence became instead a judgment on vocation, implying that farming was a waste of time for Christians.

Men and women who were thriving Christians planning to go back home to a vocation they loved became convinced that to be really serious about the Lord they needed to give up their dreams of farming.

Scott, the aspiring farmer I introduced you to in chapter 1, illustrates this kind of confused spiritual thinking that has plagued many of us in all walks of life. When Scott reflected back on his underlying assumptions, he told me, "All through my Christian life, there seems to have been a subtle selling of vocational Christian work as the crowning glory to a person's earthly existence. If I'd been really honest with myself when I was considering joining this ministry staff, I would have chosen to be a godly Christian farmer. But I felt guilty thinking that, as though farming was a second-rate option, undeserving of God's interest or blessing."

Scott went on, "I've heard it said that if Monday morning is the worst part of your job and Friday evening is the best, then you're in the wrong job! Well, I must be in the wrong job. I don't think the ministry is meant to feel like a daily grind of obedience when deep down, I'd rather be serving the Lord out of desire from the top of a haystack."

Do you hear the false guilt and confusion in Scott's original decision to "sell the farm" and enter the ministry, his deep-seated notion that God really values the one who does the "good" work rather than the "less-good" work? Ideas like that creep in easily. And when they take hold, they spawn a string of other errors. First we think God's favor rests only on "sacred" work. Then we start believing that sacrifice and commitment belong only to the realm of the "Christian worker."

In reality, spiritual maturity means that on some level, you can trust the desires God has given you. If you've committed your life to Jesus Christ, then the desires planted in your head and taking root in your heart may very well be the first fruits of your future career direction. "Love God and do as you please," John Wesley said, meaning that your longings and desires are there for a reason you would do well not to ignore.

Are you drawn to teaching or farming or financial investing or preaching? It's likely that you're being drawn by God. Look at your job as the tremendous spiritual opportunity it really is. Choosing the job you long to do may be the most far-reaching commitment to Christ you can make.

"If we love the Lord and we love our work, then our lives

will attract others to the Lord of our work." That principle liberates. Living in this kind of freedom can happen when you find your place.

FULL TIME IN THE LORD'S WORK

"Any work done for the Lord becomes the work of the Lord." Do you believe this statement? I mean, *really* believe it?

That's what Larry Peabody asserts in his book *Secular Work is Full-Time Service.*[3] I think he's right. Anyone submitted to Christ is a "full-time Christian worker," a priest in work clothes.

I love the contribution that I get to make to God's world by helping to unleash His people to become what they're designed to be. I enjoy watching the metamorphosis in a person's thinking when she realizes that her God-given strengths afford her a spiritual opportunity right there in the marketplace.

Look over my shoulder with me at a letter from a man who wrote about that kind of moment—when all of a sudden he saw his life, his job, as an integral part of something much larger than himself. I heard from Ken after he had attended a "Great Niche Hunt" seminar in which we exploded the myth of secular versus sacred work:

> My public relations job began last December—and within a month, I knew I would love this job. In fact, I loved it so much I almost felt guilty—like I ought to squeeze in as many Christian activities during the evenings as I could to thank God for how He blessed me.
>
> In the past I felt that I ought to become a missionary so I could "really serve God." But this morning as I was driving to work, it hit me—I *am* a missionary! Not in the usual definition of going to a foreign country, but in the sense that now all of my life, including my work, is God's revealed mission field for

me. My strengths are intended for active use in my career—right now!

Identifying the falsehood in the "secular versus sacred" concept helped me understand that the hours I spend on a job are no more secular than the lunches, dinners, and other activities that build the friendships upon which the gospel travels.

Someday I may really go overseas as a tent-making missionary. But I have great peace now in knowing that all I'm doing in my life—not just evenings and weekends—is within God's plan and bringing glory to Him.

Indeed, somewhere along the line, we've got to recover the old Puritan concept of the "sanctity of vocation." Each of us has a vocation, a holy niche in the overall scheme of things, that is given to us by God.

When we're in our natural niche, some pretty supernatural things can happen. I think of Cy, a friend of mine who spent a summer commuting from Chicago to New Jersey every week to work on a stressful project for AT&T. After it was all over he was sharing with a nonChristian coworker about his struggles to maintain the focus of his spiritual life during that time.

His friend responded, "It's obvious to those of us around you that your life is grounded spiritually in God—and honestly, we find it attractive." Those were his friend's very words!

"What I'm beginning to realize," Cy says now, "is that often while I feel like I'm just trying to walk with God through the mundane, supernatural things are happening I can't even begin to see."

When I consider the importance of our work lives, a scene from the movie *Dead Poets Society* comes to mind. Prep school English teacher John Keating leads his class of youths out into the hall to look at photographs of trophy-winning school athletes, all long dead.

The boys stare rather blankly into the glass case. Then Keating leans in over their shoulders and whispers in a mesmerizing tone, provocative yet to the point, "*Carpe diem. Seize the day.*"

What a graphic way to remind someone that life is short! This is no dress rehearsal. There is a big, needy world waiting for us to make the contribution for which God has especially equipped us. And if we've determined to be God's man or woman, then our contribution will be a ministry—whether it's made from a pulpit or a pigpen.

The Common Tasks
The common tasks are beautiful if we
Have eyes to see their shining ministry.
The plowman with his share deep in the loam;
The carpenter whose skilled hands build a home;
The gardener working with reluctant sod,
Faithful to his partnership with God—
These are the artisans of life. And, oh,
A woman with her eyes and cheeks aglow,
Watching a kettle, tending a scarlet flame,
Guarding a little child—there is no name
For these great ministries, and eyes are dull
That do not see that they are beautiful;
That do not see within the common tasks
The simple answer to the thing God asks
Of any child, a pride within His breast;
That at our given work we do our best.

—Grace Noll Crowell[4]

CHAPTER THREE

THE STEWARDSHIP OF SELF
Who You Are and Why It Matters

> Men go abroad to wonder at the height of mountains,
> at the huge waves of the sea, at the long courses of the rivers,
> at the vast compass of the ocean, at the circular motion of the stars;
> and they pass by themselves without wondering.
>
> **Saint Augustine[1]**

A young man came into my office to confide in me his troubling situation at work. Rich was so ashamed that he could barely get the words out.

As he looked down at the carpet, his eyes studying its weave, he told me about his recent demotion from a managerial position in a large manufacturing firm. He had been reassigned to a maintenance job in a move designed to quietly force him out of the company.

Rich had taken the manager's job simply because he had found out from a friend that it was available. Once in it, he realized he missed the structure and predictability he'd enjoyed during his preceding years as a supply officer in the Army. But he hadn't expected to fail at the new position. And he was surprised that he preferred the position he'd been demoted to—he enjoyed maintaining the machinery out back!

When he finished his story, he raised his eyes from the floor and looked at me imploringly. "Where do I go from here?" he asked. "What kind of jobs are available to a person with a good Army record who's a crummy people manager?"

Rich obviously believed that I could help him. But the assistance I had to offer him was not the help he thought he wanted—though it was just the help he needed.

"Well," I started off, "you've come to the wrong place to ask about specific jobs—but that's good. You see, your real problem is that you're a poem without rhyme."

Now when I say profoundly ambigous statements like that, I sit back and wait. I know what's coming.

First, I see my friends or clients frown. I watch them squint their eyes and roll those words around in their minds like stray marbles. I know they're stifling the urge to spit them back out at me with a big *"What?"*

I waited until Rich went through these gyrations, then continued. "Each of us is a product of God's self-expression. When Paul wrote his now-famous letter many years ago to fellow Christians living in Ephesus, he said that we are God's workmanship, created in Christ Jesus to do good works, which God prepared in advance for us to do."

Rich was still squinting.

"The word Paul used that we translate as 'workmanship' comes from the same Greek root, *poiema,* from which we derive our word *poem,*" I went on. "In a very real sense, you and I are God's poetry in motion, His artistic self-expression designed to reflect His image in certain ways in His world. There is 'rhyme and reason' to the way you've been designed to function. It just seems," I added, "that you have yet to discover your rhyme."

Rich nodded. "That's for sure!" he broke in.

"You were hoping to find a career and placement counselor who could tell you what jobs are out there, weren't you?" I said. "But that's the route that rode you right into a managerial job you hated—and your underlings probably didn't like you in it, either. Am I right?"

He nodded again. He was following me now.

"I would venture to say that your greatest mistake was not in the realm of managing people, but in your failure to manage yourself—your vocational self. It sounds as though you entered the job market out of the military like a kid who closed his eyes and grabbed the first pair of pants he found in his drawer, only to discover he couldn't get both legs inside."

Here our conversation broke wide open. I loved it! Bit by bit, the loose and seemingly unconnected threads of Rich's life started weaving into a discernible pattern. Yes, he liked shop in high school. There in companionable solitude he could watch something take shape with his "hands on" the project. Being a supply officer might bore others, but he enjoyed monitoring the details of a job that had a clear-cut beginning and end.

On and on he went, sharing the activities and accomplishments he had gravitated toward from his youth on. Over the course of a few hours we were able to sketch a much better picture of what Rich had to offer as an individual scouting out the work place. It became crystal clear that his orientation was toward working with information and things—not with or through people.

Now you may say, "That conclusion is so obvious that no one should need more than a minute of introspection and dialogue to discover it. What's the big deal?"

I can only answer from what I've seen in years of helping others piece together an accurate representation of who they are. As Rich's story reveals—and as I believe the Bible tells us—we are often the most blind to the clearest realities concerning ourselves. We don't know ourselves—not spiritually, not relationally, not vocationally. Most of us do a lot of stumbling around in the dark.

Rich's "failure" in managing people actually proved to be his saving grace. Like my own crisis over Bryan's death, this was his wake-up call. It provided a revelation about himself that he had not seen before.

Once he began to see what he enjoyed and was drawn to, once he could call those desires legitimate—then he was halfway home. He could start to own himself—his vocational self—which is a crucial step toward finding one's real niche in the world of work.

A SUITABLE SEARCH

Now all of this talk about discovering self can make a person a bit uneasy. If that's true for you, perhaps that's because, as Christians, we tend to confuse *self-assessment* with *self-centeredness.*

"Didn't Jesus teach that I save my life by losing it, that the object of following Him is to deny myself?" we question under our breath.

To which I add another question: Which part of yourself did Jesus tell you to deny? The part that was made in the image of your Creator or the part that was tainted by the Fall?

You are God's creation, made in a unique way. *Your* ability to design, to understand, to care for, to steward and appreciate the resources and people and knowledge around you, is one of your principle means of honoring the One who made you that way—the One who gave you *those* abilities.

"I don't know about all these tests and assessments that make us focus on ourselves," questioned one thoughtful woman during a "Great Niche Hunt" workshop. "It seems more humanistic than Christian to be so self-concerned."

But a cause for real distress, as this woman came to realize, is not our desire to know ourselves, but our failure to deny our sin. We confuse our lust and selfishness, our malice and determined independence, with ourselves as we were made in His image. And in so doing, we deny what we should embrace and hold on to what we should release.

To know your "self," in the vocational sense, is the process of discovering who you are and what you have to offer, so that you can be a better steward of the way God made you. It's a practical means of acknowledging the image of God planted in your soul, of fleshing out the truth that you were made a little lower than the angels and crowned with glory and honor (Psalm 8:3-6).

We need only turn back to Genesis to see that when we ignore or overlook the individual tailoring of our creation, we make less of God. As the Hebrew words and images in these opening scenes reveal, here is an Artist who gathers common clay and fashions a masterpiece. The rest of creation unfolds at the command of a word—but with humanity, God uses painstaking care. Other animals have the breath of life; we alone have the breath of God.

Who you are and how you are designed matters—immensely so. Jesus is the consummate example of someone who knew who He was and who lived within the freedom of those boundaries. Christ refused the temptation to be what He was not: a political guru who could overthrow Rome, a showman, a respectable member of the Sanhedrin. He knew that the life He had to give came out of obedience to who He truly was—God Incarnate. Only in offering that true self did He have anything to give.

I am deeply challenged by Christ's determination to offer the essence of who He was. When I apply His example to the realm of work I realize that in reality, all I actually have to give is who I am created to be. Whatever else I try to offer will not, in the long run, be much of a contribution. To give out of a false image of myself will drain me and dwarf others. As someone once said, "If you'll take care of doing your thing, I'll be freed up to do mine."

THE PITFALLS OF NOT GOING YOUR OWN WAY

Throughout all of your life, you've been drawn, as if by an unseen magnet, to certain ways of operating. Perhaps you haven't been able to identify those repeated patterns of your functioning—but they've been there nonetheless.

The truth of who you are as an individual is hard to

ignore. But some of us manage well enough to avoid it in practice—with some predictable results.

BOREDOM

When you get stuck in a job you don't belong in, you'll soon start feeling like a hamster on a treadmill—even if the work itself is challenging.

Boredom is one of the more accurate indicators that the work you've chosen leaves the most essential parts of you untouched. It has little to do with skill. You may be well qualified for the job, even apparently successful at it—yet you're "bored out of your gourd." The work just doesn't tap into your motivation for contributing to your world.

"I got a degree in accounting," said one discontent woman, "because everyone said I should do something practical in the business world. For several years I've put in my time in a large accounting firm, each day not wanting to get out of bed to go to work. I can do the job, but I hate it. I am always drawn to the things that influence and allow me to interact with people more. It's the creative side of me that feels so stifled."

She described the daily grind: "In my job I sit in a little cubicle, working in straight lines with numbers, having very little interaction with others. I feel like I'm in jail. And if you try to get creative as an accountant, jail is where you wind up!"

BURNOUT

When we're well matched to our jobs, we can be emotionally energized even when physically exhausted. When we're mismatched, our jobs can slowly, sometimes imperceptibly, drain us of our emotional vitality. Once we detect the leak, it's often too late to patch it up. It can feel as if our very lives went down that drain.

When we go on long enough in a job that doesn't fit our design and desires—long enough to lose heart for the ideals or opportunities that may have been originally inviting—we quite often enter an emotional wasteland referred to as "burnout."

The kind of burnout I'm referring to happens not when we're overworked, but wrongly worked. The direction of our investment is off center. Perhaps when this occurs we've been following a path that we let someone else steer us on.

A friend who recently regained a sense of personal balance described it this way: "It's like pushing up the wrong hill so long that even if you reach the top of what's expected of you, it doesn't match what you wanted to accomplish."

Psychologist Douglas LaBier began to note the increasing frequency with which his clients' troubles seemed to stem directly from their work lives. In his book *Modern Madness: The Emotional Fallout of Success,* he described the toll exacted by the pressure to be what you aren't: "[F]or most, the price of molding oneself too much to 'fit in' or 'look good' is a normal but troubled feeling *of being centerless, of having no self.* Many well-adapted but troubled careerists therefore feel depressed, lonely and alienated, vaguely anxious and passionless, and dissatisfied with life and success."[2]

The fine irony in failing to understand and embrace my vocational self is that I actually seem to lose myself—though not in the kind of voluntary self-giving Jesus spoke of. Rather, this loss of self is more closely akin to self-annihilation, a fundamental disregard for my created nature that leaves me feeling empty and alone and used up.

In *The Postponed Generation,* Susan Littwin quoted Robert Ehrmann, Director of the Career Development Unit at UCLA, on the result of vocational mistakes. "Our worst cases," said Ehrmann, "are those who try to make something of themselves that they are not. For instance, the writer who becomes an accountant. Or anyone who takes a pragmatic route and goes into a highly employable field where he is mismatched. These people come back disasters, emotional and physical wrecks."[3]

Isn't it amazing how God always brings us back to the

truth of how He made us? The fact that you and I have been uniquely designed and individually tailored by God is a reality we can neglect for only so long before it overtakes us.

We aren't blank slates on which any old inscription can be engraved. Job matching is not simply a function of acquiring a title and necessary skills to go along with it. We're predisposed to a particular direction; we have an aptitude for a particular style of functioning in our world; we are motivated by the dreams and desires for contribution that have been planted deep within us.

Perhaps this is part of what David had in mind when he said, "For He Himself knows our frame; He is mindful that we are but dust" (Psalm 103:14, NASB). The Hebrew word for "frame" here is best rendered "purpose." God knows the reason for which He made us, and when we search that out in the form of matching our gifts and motivations to the work world, we honor God's purpose in us. We become responsible, knowledgeable caretakers of ourselves—His representative stewards.

THE ROLE YOU PLAY

A friend of mine was telling me her struggles with career development. She was frustrated with all the effort necessary to identify her "Functional Design," explore the world of work, and clarify her own desires for contribution. In the midst of our conversation she made a comment that verbalizes a common false assumption.

"God is sovereign," my friend said, "and if I really pray about it, He won't allow me to make a poor decision and wind up in a job that I hate."

I've met a good many committed Christians who think this way. The mistaken assumption is that in sincerely appealing to God's sovereignty we can avoid human responsibility. But God is not in the business of allowing us to shirk our duties.

Part of the way we grow is by assuming stewardship

responsibility for the gifts, abilities, desires, and motivations that God has given us. Jesus clearly illustrated this responsibility when He told the parable of the talents (Matthew 25:14-30). The two servants who made a wise investment of the resources they had been given were praised. But the servant who shrank from the responsibility of investing what he had been given was harshly condemned.

I still remember the first time I really grasped the fact that no one but me had been given the authority or responsibility over my contribution to God's world of work. Others could help me, and I did enlist their aid, but ultimately the responsibility was always mine, before my Creator. At that point, I became something of a "private contractor." After I clearly identified what I had to offer and wanted to accomplish, I began surveying the world of work to see where I could invest it. I had begun to grasp the reality that we all must come to: each of us is essentially a "business of one," making our individual contribution to this world under the sponsorship of the King of the universe.

I won't mislead you. It does take effort to identify your design and clarify your desires. It's much easier to be told what to do than to make careful decisions. The world is full of people who followed the mooing herd and in the process lost their own path.

In my dealings with individuals who need to make vocational changes and choices, I sometimes have the impression that they're waiting for me to tell them what to do. "Give me some kind of test or something that will tell me exactly what I should do and become," they plead inwardly, if not openly.

"Expecting a counselor to choose a job for you is like asking a shoe salesman to pick the right shoe for you," said Rodney Laughlin in *The Job Hunter's Handbook.* "No matter how much you tell him about the size and shape of your foot, only you can tell if the shoe really fits. A counselor's primary value will be his ability to guide and encourage you. You will have to work just as hard."[4]

Rich, my ex-military friend turned "people manager,"

knew the trauma of leaving his highly regimented environment to reenter the marketplace with its multiple choices. Whether we're in transition like Rich, or in college and used to being told where to be when for the last twenty years, or in business and living for the weekend when "life" can begin, our great need is to assume the investment responsibility for what we've been entrusted to give to God's world of work.

Although we grow up wanting to measure up in other's eyes, it's neither the pressure from parents, nor the suggestions of our peers, nor the proddings of our authority figures that should determine our vocational investment.

If what the Apostle Paul says in Ephesians is true—that each of us is God's "poem"—then the principal determinant of our vocational direction must be the "rhyme and reason" of our functional selves and the desires God has put in our hearts.

POETRY IN MOTION

Our world of work is much different than the one our parents faced. Most of them acquired a profession or joined a company that carried them through their entire careers.

For our parents, living in and around World War II, the question of who they were or where they fit in the working world was not a particularly relevant one. In wartime, each person does his duty with few questions asked. Wars are won that way—when everyone does whatever needs to be done to accomplish the task. Under such circumstances, the worth of the individual is recognized but his uniqueness is surrendered to the identity and mission of the group.

Those of us in the Baby Boom generation have met with a different experience, which presents us with more options. The world seems to change underneath our feet every five years. Indeed, if the statistics are accurate, we will be changing jobs about every four years, and we will change entire career directions three or four times during our lifetime. We can hardly afford not to know who we are and what we have to contribute!

Discovering where we really fit is both possible and necessary for those of us who don't expect to be squeezing warm sand between our toes every day on a Florida beach any time soon. And as Christians, we ought to be the ones leading the pack in those kinds of internal discoveries. We should be experiencing the tremendous benefits of vocational fit as we recognize ourselves as God's creative self-expression.

It matters a great deal who you are. It matters that you steward your "self" with wisdom and informed decision-making. In your own self-expression in His world, in your work, you represent the God of all there is. You are His statement—His poetry in motion.

I hope I've convinced you by now that to know your vocational self is not only a worthwhile biblical goal, it's a practical necessity. If you're with me, read on. You're about to discover how to identify the threads in your own "Functional Design."

CHAPTER FOUR

GOING BACK FOR THE FUTURE
Your History Is Important

God does not bring interests, experiences, abilities, or
limitations into our lives capriciously, but rather, purposefully.
Consequently an examination of ourselves and our past
experiences can bring genuine insight into God's plan.

Martin E. Clark[1]

Anne grew up with a pencil in her hand and a sketch pad
on her lap. She spent hour after hour drawing designs of
model homes and their interiors. On sunny summer after-
noons, in a field of tall weeds behind her suburban home,
Anne would gather the neighborhood gang to weave grass
into forts and build "mansions" out of boxes. Long after the
other kids lost interest and went off to pursue other adven-
tures, Anne was transporting all the removable rugs and
accessories from her parent's home to furnish her newly-
built abodes.

Today Anne markets herself as an interior decorating
consultant. She has exchanged weeds and boxes for finer
working materials, but her basic love of design and order
remains the same.

When Tom was in junior high school, he was fascinated

by mechanical gadgets. "I wanted to take things apart, figure out how they worked, and then add something to them to make them work differently. It's the thrill of invention that intrigues me."

Among his early accomplishments were a motorized fish feeder, a one-way intercom he purchased and upgraded into a two-way system, a homemade satellite dish attached to his tree house, and an electronic saxophone.

Today Tom is a mechanical engineer for a respected firm, developing his own products and inventions on the side.

A fifteen-year-old boy named Chick found great delight in sneaking into the local hospital and watching surgeries. He'd slip into the nearest white lab coat he could find, pretend he was a medical student, and find a seat in the amphitheater of the operating room. Amputations, skin grafts—fascinated, he saw it all! In his neighborhood he'd watch for stray animals, give them a little ether, and practice some exploratory surgery. (Of course, he'd always sew them back up before letting them go.)

Not long ago, Chick held public office as the U.S. Surgeon General—C. Everett Koop. Perhaps you remember him in his official army uniform keeping a stern fatherly watch over the nation's health.

There's no mistaking it. Your past contains road signs that point toward your future. In some measure, you still are what you were. Despite the many ways in which you've no doubt changed, in a fundamental way you're the same as you've always been. Your mission possible—and the one I'm going to invite you to in this chapter—is to retrace the images of your own past in order to give you a much more complete picture of what your present and future ought to include.

YOUR HISTORY

Looking to the past to clarify the future is a common practice in career development. In analyzing your past accomplishments, you will discover the clues to the pattern of how God has designed you to operate in His world.

That's right—a pattern. Remember how we discussed in chapter 3 that each of us is God's workmanship—His poem? There's a pattern to the poetry of your life, rhyme and reason to the way you've always preferred to do things. It shows that you've been gifted with what I call a "Functional Design"— regardless of your background and your development as a child.

Your personal history is like a huge photo album stuffed with all sizes, shapes, and colors of snaphots showing you doing things that you enjoyed and that brought a sense of personal accomplishment and reward. These pictures of your most enjoyable accomplishments reveal the fabric of your future. Once you've discovered in them the threads of your Functional Design, you can make knowledgeable, perceptive career choices that allow you to reflect who you really are. Then you can market yourself with confidence for work that fits what God has designed you to invest.

Not long ago I led a "Great Niche Hunt" seminar in which one of the participants complained that there was nothing usable or profitable from his pre-Christian years that might help him identify his design. "I spent most of my high school and college years either doing or dealing drugs," he recalled.

Granted, this reformed drug dealer's life had been built on questionable values. But I assured him that even here, in his drug-dealing past, the pattern of his Functional Design could be uncovered.

We are creatures of design, whether we live out that design in the pursuit of godly or ungodly values. Our Functional Design is part of our creation in the image of God. It's not something we acquire after we become a Christian; nor can we turn it on and off. Our Functional Design is part of our make-up.

Together my reformed friend and I began to probe into his history for mental snaphots of himself involved in enjoyable accomplishments. For example, he had always been an avid reader. In the ninth grade he had read more books than anyone in his class. He'd chaired library committees that helped to select new books. Even in his drug days he'd read numerous books on how to grow and harvest marijuana crops.

A common thread we discovered in his "album" was reading and researching information. When I pointed this out, he responded enthusiastically, "You know, that's right! One of my favorite hobbies even now is to go to the library and just browse for hours through books."

We also uncovered a lifelong pattern of influencing people by recruiting them to join his various ventures. In grade school he was the ringleader of the neighborhood gang. In junior high he got himself elected to student government, gathering quite a following in the process. During his years of pushing drugs, he had the largest "sole proprietorship" in the city, having recruited a number of "subcontractors" to deal for him. Though a dubious accomplishment indeed, he'd been hugely successful at getting others involved in his trade.

From every moral standpoint, his drug years had been a loss. Yet even here in this useless wasteland, the pattern of his poetry revealed a certain rhyme with other periods of his life. Underneath the trash in his life I was able to find the treasure of his unique Functional Design.

Perhaps you, too, will need to wipe away a certain amount of grime that coats your life as a fallen person living in a fallen world. But look beneath it: You may find a good picture of the Functional Design that your Creator has placed in trust with you to invest in His world.

"What's so special about dinky little stories from my past?" you may be wondering. Perhaps more than you thought. Remember the hours you spent shaping pots out of red Georgia clay? Or the stamp collection you added to for years? Memories like these hold the keys to your functional future.

The rest of this chapter is designed to help you open the photo album of your past and observe yourself in action. In the next three chapters, I'll help you piece together these snap-shots to create the full montage of your Functional Design.

A WHOLE LIFE RESUME

What have you done in life that you've really enjoyed doing and that gave you a sense of personal accomplishment and reward?

This question operates as a screening device as you flip through the mental pictures of your past. You're looking for accomplishments, not just experiences. What have you accomplished that you found both enjoyable and rewarding?

While answering this question for me one day, a friend of mine in his early forties said, "You know, mostly what I remember about my childhood was collecting the caps from pop bottles and playing army with them. That doesn't seem like much of an accomplishment. What's so great about that?"

"Nothing!" I responded. "Absolutely worthless—except for the fact that within that play I'll bet we'll be able to see some of your Functional Design peeking through."

Indeed we did. This friend of mine loves to give direction to groups of people these days. And he likes to come up with that direction on his own, with little input or interaction from others. He enjoys developing a master plan, a strategy, then informing the "troops" of what will be expected of them. That's exactly what we saw him doing with his bottle cap "army guys"—a pattern we traced from his current situation all the way back to the roots of his childhood.

So make sure you consider every realm of your life. Each has the potential to uncover important clues—in hob-bies, school, social activities, vacations, family life, other sorts of relationships, volunteer activities, home ownership, church activities, as well as on the job. In *What Color Is Your Parachute?* Richard Bolles divides life into three realms for exploration—leisure, learning, and labor.[2] If that structure helps, use it.

If you're like most of my clients, it's best if you'll start the search through your mental picture album with the recent past. Starting there is like jump starting a dead car on a cold winter morning—it gives just the right kick to get going toward your destination. And like my Grandpa Cowan once said when I was having trouble getting motivated to do something—"If you don't never get started you ain't never gonna get to where you was wantin' to be!"

From your most recent history you'll want to page back through the images in your memory toward your childhood. Each era of your life contains important pictures that make a valuable contribution to the collage of the "functional you." What will eventually emerge as you put these pictures into words is an autobiographical montage of a lifetime of enjoyable activities and accomplishments, a "Whole Life Resume."

It's been suggested by others who help people recall the good things of their past that if you're not much at writing, perhaps you ought to tell your stories to a tape recorder and then get them transcribed (a fairly inexpensive process).

Here are some ground rules for getting your mental pictures on paper.

Ground Rules for Photo Hunting

■ *Record activities that show yourself in action accomplishing something.*

If you engaged in this activity in a group context, describe your role within the group. If this was a long-term activity (such as a lifelong love and habit of reading), then list it as such. Describe each activity in just one sentence—what I call a "story line."

■ *Record only activities that were enjoyable to you.*

The fact that Aunt Susie thought you were her best little artist means very little if you really would rather have been out fixing your bike.

No one is going to grade this activity or reprimand

you for feeling a greater sense of personal accomplishment and reward from redecorating your house than from leading a Bible study group. Be honest about what you really *enjoy* doing.
- *The activities you record need not have "earthshaking" value.*

The details of your play with toy soldiers when you were a kid are just as important as what you did last year in the corporate world.

Overall, remember, the important thing is that any activity you put to paper should meet these three qualifications: (1) it was genuinely enjoyable for you, (2) it shows you in action moving toward some result, and (3) it brought you a sense of personal accomplishment and reward.

Take a look at the following list of accomplishment activities compiled from the Whole Life Resumes of several of my clients. I've included these actual responses to jog your thinking about areas you might otherwise overlook. Use the list to expand the boundaries of what you might consider worthy data from your past.

**Case Study Examples
of What Some People Have Considered Fun**
- Created battle scenes with huge armies of toy soldiers
- Collected pictures I drew of make-believe bums
- Made and mastered the use of a slingshot
- Mastered every job given to me as an employee of a restaurant
- Befriended the new kid at school and developed a best friendship
- Won top honors in a debate contest
- In two weeks learned what it took the rest of the class an entire semester to understand

- Built a tree house from remains of a torn-down cottage on our farm
- Tutored special education students
- Team taught a twelve-week series on "Stress" at a large church
- Trained for and competed in my first marathon
- Created a seventy-page notebook for A/V training at a major conference center
- Shot photojournalism story of men playing tennis
- Read sixty books in one summer
- Determined the differences between alligators and crocodiles by sitting near their cage in the zoo and observing them
- Put ten years worth of family photos into albums in chronological sequence
- Designed and marketed my own series of greeting cards
- Played the part of a villainess for a melodrama in a talent show
- By hard work and practice worked my way up the tennis team ladder to number two position and co-captain status
- Earned rank as Eagle Scout and was elected senior patrol leader
- Befriended an international student and helped him become acquainted with American culture
- Designed a way to hook up my saxophone to electricity
- Befriended the toughest girl on the floor and recruited her to Christ
- Coordinated the details of the office in such a way that it won my boss and myself a promotion
- Drove six people home from college in a Ford Pinto through a major Minnesota snowstorm on an interstate highway that was closed to traffic

Note: With enough individuals, this list could go on forever. The variety of activities that people enjoy and gain
a sense of accomplishment and reward from is virtually
inexhaustible. Isn't it great!

WRITING YOUR STORY LINES

Now, beginning with the decade of your current age and
working back toward your childhood (use these categories: 70s, 60s, 50s, 40s, 30s, 20s, Teens, Childhood), list
three to five story-line summaries of things you've enjoyed
accomplishing in each general period of your life.

By the way, nobody is too young or too old for this exercise. I got a letter not long ago from a seventy-seven-year-
old friend who just landed a job that has her going around
speaking to the elderly in Florida's mobile home parks in an
effort to get them to "stop being couch potatoes and meet the
world once more." She ends the letter this way: "Just wanted
you to know that it is possible to find your niche even at
seventy-seven."

Story Lines

Era of your life _____   Era of your life _____

■   ■

■   ■

■   ■

■   ■

■   ■

Story Lines

Era of your life _____

■

■

■

■

■

Era of your life _____

■

■

■

■

■

Era of your life _____

■

■

■

■

■

Era of your life _____

■

■

■

■

■

Era of your life _____

■

■

■

■

■

Era of your life _____

■

■

■

■

■

After you've compiled a healthy list of story lines, *pick seven* that you consider most important to you. On the next few pages you will explore each of these seven story lines in more detail. Each exploration will compose what I call an "Action Shot." Once you complete these seven comprehensive Action Shots, you'll use them later in chapter 7 to determine all the specific components of your unique Functional Design.

The first Action Shot has been filled in with sample answers as an example of how to expand a Story Line.

ACTION SHOT EXAMPLE

Story Line: **Era of your life** _20s_

Took hundreds of slides and developed slide shows to promote activities.

A. How did you get started in this?

My dad is a very active amateur photographer. I grew up watching slide shows. I began to develop a critical eye—seeing what captured my imagination, what left me cold. Began to toy with photography as a way to express myself—a way to show others the world in ways they hadn't noticed. In my previous job as a campus minister, I incorporated the use of photography into much of what I did.

B. What were the specifics of what you actually did?

Used my camera in my work-role of promoting Christian ministry on a college campus. For every activity the university hosted, I became the unofficial, official photographer. I'd gather photos of student life, dorm rooms, classrooms, etc. I wanted to capture the details of everything that meant student life. In most cases I was looking for the unique shot, the one that the average photographer would overlook. I wanted each of my photos to make a lasting impression, to gain immediate crowd reaction.

I've used my photography to promote a number of activities. I've become known to my friends and coworkers as the "Picture Man" . . . the slide show specialist. Some of my work has been used by others in newsletters and brochures. I do best when I can create the scene. I hate "canned" photography. I don't do well when someone wants me to come to their house and take photos of their family and dog sitting in front of the fireplace. Yuck!

On a trip to Europe with friends, I was asked to shoulder the job of official photographer. I stuffed my camera bag with film and captured the uniqueness of life there as I saw it. The variety of restroom facilities we encountered provided for some interesting shots.

I've always found myself drawn most to shots that fill the whole frame with clusters or groups of things—or perhaps a close-up on a face or object. I have a great shot of 150 candy bars of different names all heaped in a pile. I call it "Local Bars." It's always good for a few "snickers" in a slide show. Another shot shows just the back of a man's head, very close up. The texture is awesome! I'm fascinated by the blend of the parts of something that integrate themselves together into the whole.

After getting the slides back from processing, I would carefully label them and put them in various slide boxes. I've always wanted to know where things are and be able to get them at a moment's notice. I'd categorize the slides and code them by activity and date. When time came to put together a slide show, I'd be able to pull things together chronologically.

C. What aspects of this activity gave you the greatest sense of personal accomplishment and reward?

I liked capturing things on film that made people laugh or gasp or wonder how I got that shot. I liked collecting information about things or people that others didn't see. I liked presenting the best or most entertaining truth about something. I liked the reputation that I built, becoming known as the expert. I liked being called upon to lend my photographic expertise to some project.

D. What would have made this activity even more rewarding for you?

I would really have enjoyed being able to sell more of my photographs for publication in magazines, etc. I tried to market them through an agency, but no one was buying.

As I mentioned, some of my work was used in brochures put together by others. Having had more of my work used that way—being able to see it actually used in other publications with my name attached—would have been very rewarding. And being paid at the same time would have been the ultimate!

ACTION SHOT ONE

Story Line: **Era of your life** _____

A. How did you get started in this?

B. What were the specifics of what you actually did?

C. What aspects of this activity gave you the greatest sense of personal accomplishment and reward?

D. What would have made this activity even more rewarding for you?

ACTION SHOT TWO

Story Line: **Era of your life _____**

A. How did you get started in this?

B. What were the specifics of what you actually did?

C. What aspects of this activity gave you the greatest sense of personal accomplishment and reward?

D. What would have made this activity even more rewarding for you?

ACTION SHOT THREE

Story Line: **Era of your life** _____

A. How did you get started in this?

B. What were the specifics of what you actually did?

C. What aspects of this activity gave you the greatest sense of personal accomplishment and reward?

D. What would have made this activity even more rewarding for you?

ACTION SHOT FOUR

Story Line: **Era of your life** _____

A. How did you get started in this?

B. What were the specifics of what you actually did?

C. What aspects of this activity gave you the greatest sense of personal accomplishment and reward?

D. What would have made this activity even more rewarding for you?

ACTION SHOT FIVE

Story Line: **Era of your life** _____

A. How did you get started in this?

B. What were the specifics of what you actually did?

C. What aspects of this activity gave you the greatest sense of personal accomplishment and reward?

D. What would have made this activity even more rewarding for you?

ACTION SHOT SIX

Story Line: **Era of your life** _____

A. How did you get started in this?

B. What were the specifics of what you actually did?

C. What aspects of this activity gave you the greatest sense of personal accomplishment and reward?

D. What would have made this activity even more rewarding for you?

ACTION SHOT SEVEN

Story Line: **Era of your life** _____

A. How did you get started in this?

B. What were the specifics of what you actually did?

C. What aspects of this activity gave you the greatest sense of personal accomplishment and reward?

D. What would have made this activity even more rewarding for you?

THE NEXT STEP

"All the world's a stage," declared Jaques in Shakespeare's *As You Like It*, "and all the men and women merely players: They have their exits and their entrances; and one man in his time plays many parts."

The historical data of your enjoyable accomplishments reveals the "many parts" of the life you've been living. Perhaps for the moment they seem a bit disjointed, as if there is no clear flow or pattern to what you've done and accomplished that might lead you into the future.

Not to worry! In chapters 5 and 6 you'll discover a model for understanding the "rhyme and reason" of your past accomplishments. In chapter 7 you'll apply the model to your stories to piece together the picture of the real you in action.

So hang in there. Be sure to do your best at completing your seven action shots in this chapter before moving on. The familiar adage of "garbage in, garbage out" brought to us by the computer world applies here as well. The better the data you take with you into this next step in your niche hunt, the better will be your results.

CHAPTER FIVE

PREFERRED STYLES
What Do You Bring to the World of Work?

If you paint a house with a hammer, the hammer suffers—not to mention the poor house! There's a tool that the tool maker has styled specifically for painting. It's called a brush. I've met a lot of hammers who have been trying to paint houses, and a lot of brushes who have been trying to pound nails. In both cases, the results have been less than good.

From "The Great Niche Hunt" Seminar

When my son was seven years old he devised an ingenious plan to save himself time and trouble. Before he kissed his mother and me good night each evening, he would carefully lay out his clothes for the next day. Then right before he slipped into bed, he would change into his next-day outfit. As soon as he opened his eyes the following morning, he was ready to go!

Naturally, we were concerned. So, as good parents should do when their children adopt strange habits, we asked him to explain his reasoning.

He had it all figured out. "Dad," he answered, "if I get dressed for school the night before, then all I have to do the next morning is brush my teeth and comb my hair and I'm ready!" How could I argue with such a strategy? He was getting a jump on his day. New opportunities were his in

75

the morning just because he was dressing for his day the night before. He had time to watch cartoons, play with his G.I. Joes, and eat an extra bowl of cereal before he left for school.

As far as I could see, there was only one problem with his system: he stunk! If I allowed him to continue his new practice, the opportunities he had gained would soon be outweighed by the friendships he would lose.

LOOK BEFORE YOU LEAP

Many people approach their entry into the working world much like my son treated getting ready for his day. *They leap at the opportunity structure that lies before them without considering the person they bring to it.* And, just like my son, their results can be disastrous.

Elizabeth, the woman in my fellowship group who changed her college major from theater to economics, is miserable after several years of selling insurance. She actually belongs in the entertainment business. Everything she's ever really enjoyed doing points in that direction.

In college, Elizabeth started off following her instincts. She loved costumes and performing and getting audiences to laugh. But then she began to weigh the high cost of her degree against the riskiness of her desires. She factored in her wish to appear successful to the authority figures in her life, along with the impracticality of a performing career. And then Elizabeth fled the theater—to what seemed to be the safe haven of a degree in economics from a business school. Several years later, the "safe haven" became stifling.

Elizabeth had prepared herself to make a living—nothing wrong here. However, she chose a course based on a perceived path to success with little regard for her own aptitudes and desires. In a sense, she allowed what was "out there" to dictate her direction, rather than holding firm to what God had put "within her" to give. Elizabeth is an artist's brush who has spent years trying to pound nails!

Whatever the reason, many of us do wind up in jobs that cut against our God-given grain. Now, I'm quick to admit that there is a time and place for a "survival job." Sometimes our major employment objective goes no further than simple survival. The job may leave us as cold as yesterday's oatmeal—but it keeps our cash flow problem under control. My point is that we ought to be the first to recognize that reality because we know enough about ourselves to understand what a good job fit might really look like for us. We know where we are and where we ought to be heading.

So before I raise your expectations to an unrealistic height, let me emphasize that no job is perfect; no career path is without a few jagged spots. The figure that I help people aim for in job satisfaction is 80 percent, meaning that at least four fifths of what is required in your job matches what you have to give. Then it's quite possible for hobbies and outside interests to provide an outlet for the other 20 percent of your gifts and abilities.

In the preceding chapter we talked about how your history of enjoyable accomplishments plays an important role in discerning your vocational future. Now that you've worked your way through the process of recording your historical data of enjoyable accomplishments, you've no doubt begun to identify consistent themes—the patterns of how you prefer to function in your world. You're beginning to see threads of common colors in your historical tapestry.

As you begin to see these patterns, you will need categories, some sort of structure that will allow you to make organized sense of what you're learning about yourself. You are, after all, designed in the image of the One who brought structure to the original chaos! You are a creature designed for ordering your world.

In this chapter and the next we will develop such a structure—a model for understanding who you are in relation to the world of work. I call that model your Functional Design. It is the optimal way you are created to function.

Your Functional Design is a unique blend of preferred styles and investments. Within your preferred styles, there are specific ways in which you best:

■ Process information.
■ Solve problems.
■ Provide structure.
■ Influence people.

In these next two chapters, we will be investigating both your preferred styles and your preferred investments so that in chapter 7, you can begin to decipher the scheme of your own "poem."

PREFERRED STYLES

Processing Information

When you think of "processing information" you may well conjure images of someone punching long lines of words and numbers into a desktop computer that produces a detailed report at the push of a button. If so, put your mind at ease.

Think, for a minute, of the beginning of creation and how God operated in that setting. Genesis 1:4 says that God saw the light that He had created and He pronounced it good. We can define the style in which we "process information" as the way we gain awareness and form a conclusion—in other words, perception and judgment.

Information provides the facts and fabric of life. All that exists is identified, defined, and communicated by information. As creatures designed in God's image, we have been designed with built-in "information processing devices"—brains. Everyone's brain facilitates the common functions of gathering information and rendering judgment, yet each person's brain does so in its own uniquely programmed style.

We've all met people who liked to discover their world and come to conclusions about it in ways different from our own. Some people gain awareness of their world with a kind of "hands-on" approach where they try things and learn by doing—trial and error. Others are particularly attuned to observe the intuitive, nonverbal clues before them. Still others prefer reading and studying as primary ways to acquire information.

As an example, I'll explain how I was able to help two partners in a consulting firm discover their unique ways of processing information and thus maximize their contribution to their jobs.

Richard is an avid reader. His detailed history of enjoyable accomplishments shows a lifelong attraction to the written page. He stays on top of all the new thinking, the new laws, and all the written information in his field. When the trade journals come to the office, Richard now makes it an established part of his job routine to read them cover to cover. He loves it, but had felt guilty about taking the time for it until I helped him recognize it as a significant contribution to the team's effectiveness.

Bill, on the other hand, enjoys observing and listening as his main way of gathering an awareness of the world around him. He much prefers to read people, not words. In round table discussions, which the two of them host for work teams of other companies, Bill enjoys being able to observe interactions between participants, listen in on conversations, and watch them as they seek to accomplish certain tasks.

Richard keeps Bill informed about what he's read that relates to their business. Bill keeps Richard informed about what he's observed that relates to their clients. When they make judgments, Richard moves toward comparison of all the pros and cons of the issue. Bill usually tends to go by an intuitive sense of rightness based on what he has observed.

When careful analysis of facts is needed, Richard leads the process. When interpreting what people are feeling, Bill's opinion speaks loudest. They've come to rely on each other's gifts in this realm.

Style of Processing Information
Perception (gaining awareness)
■ Interacting/discussing
■ Observing/listening
■ Doing/trying
■ Fact finding/data collecting
■ Imagining/envisioning
■ Other . . .

Judgment (drawing conclusions)
■ Analyzing
■ Evaluating
■ Interpreting
■ Other . . .

Problem Solving

All purposeful functioning in this world is a matter of problem solving. By *problems* I don't mean "sources of perplexity, distress, or vexation," as *Webster* defines them—even though that may describe your circumstances at times. For our purposes here, a problem exists whenever a person seeks a means toward some end, a way to accomplish any goal or result.

God is a problem solver, and He displays three broad styles. He is an originator-inventor, a developer-extender, and a reproducer-maintainer.

1. Originality and invention. That God is an originator-inventor is obvious from the Bible's opening statement: "In the beginning God created the heavens and the earth." Origination and invention were at their zenith. In this context we will define originality and invention as the process of introducing the new, the different, the unique into being.

In or around 1770 a fellow named William Addis of Great Britain found himself in a cell in England's Newgate Prison for having started a riot. Frustrated with how his life was going and having little to do but think, he thought about what he'd do for a living once he got out. One day while cleaning his teeth with a rag it occured to him that there might be a better way. Saving a bone from a meal, he bored holes in it. Then he acquired bristles from the guard, cut-tied-and-glued it all together, and introduced a new product to the world.

Just a short time after his release, this "down in the mouth" jailbird launched a very successful business manufacturing his "down in the mouth" invention, the world's first toothbrush. William Addis was an originator-inventor.

My friend Elizabeth is primarily an originator-inventor. Her head swims with an incredible array of new ideas. She carries around in her head title and content ideas for a variety of children's books. Clever slogans for various political leaders slip in and out of her consciousness. On any given weekend you might find her putting together a script for her newest party idea. Although she continues to function within what to her is the confining world of insurance selling, she has created clever word pictures and presentations that allow her to explain and communicate insurance coverage possibilities to her clients.

2. *Development and extension.* God is also a developer-extender. He originated the earth, then developed things into full bloom. He planted seeds in His garden, then cultivated them with rain and sunshine. He introduced human beings to His world, then refined them through His discipline. He introduced language, then modified its application at the tower of Babel.

A friend of mine named Gary fits the description of a developer-extender. He's always enjoyed taking what's there and modifying it to make it better. Left in charge of the worship service one weekend at his church, he brought change to bear upon everything involved from the color of the bulletins to the final Amen. His hope was to improve upon what existed to make it better.

Gary derives special pleasure in taking the ideas of

others, finding their common ground, then integrating and developing them into his own approach to teach others. When he picked up the latest bestselling book on counseling, he read one on biblical interpretation at the same time to see how their concepts fit together. He's always looking for ways to enlarge and extend his own understanding of life, integrating new thoughts into his world view. Progressive change and development is familiar, even desired, territory for him.

3. Reproduction and maintenance. God is a reproducer-maintainer in the way He follows patterns that He has already established. We know that the sun will rise in the morning at a predictable time. We can be sure that rocks will fall down, not up. And we can count on small children whining at five o'clock until they get dinner. That's the way life is, because God created laws of nature.

When an individual shows preference toward the reproduction-maintenance aspect of problem solving, he feels at home in situations that give him an orderly, consistent agenda. He wants to bring solutions to bear upon problems by perpetuating a pattern already set in motion. His *modus operandi* moves toward sameness and consistency. Change is usually difficult for him both to initiate and to endure.

Bill had always fantasized being an entrepreneur in the business community—until he tried it. Carving out a share of the market for frozen yogurt, he quickly realized, was not for him. The lack of a pattern to follow left him feeling like he wasn't accomplishing a thing. He eventually hired on as a consultant, presenting success seminars created by his company to client organizations someone else has recruited. "I know exactly what I'm supposed to say every time I get before an audience," explained Bill. "I enjoy the structure. I don't need to invent it; I just want to follow it."

Ben is fascinated by figuring out how things work, and then keeping them going. He gravitates toward proven formulas that tend to produce standardized results. Today he is a highly valued part of a team that keeps a major conference center "well-oiled and working."

In His work in the world, God expresses all three types of problem solving. Each style is important in our world of work, but each needs to be invested in contexts appropriate for results required or preferred.

My wife functions as an interior decorator. Anne enjoys designing floor plans, envisioning color combinations, creating beauty and improving what exists. People call upon her gifts to change and enhance their environments. Maintaining the status quo has never been her preferred style of problem solving. It's easy to see that her preferences lean toward a blend of development-extension and originality-invention.

The work Anne does clearly would be impossible if God had not designed people who incline toward reproduction-maintenance. Imagine the frustration of hanging wallpaper that was supposed to match, but didn't—or purchasing two cans of paint with the same name on the outside but different colors on the inside. Chaos! Fortunately, the manufacturers of the supplies my wife recommends to her clients spend a great deal of time getting things just right. They are consistent throughout.

As you work through the assessment exercise in chapter 7 you will discover whether your preferences lie in originality-invention, development-extension, or reproduction-maintenance. Satisfaction in your vocational pursuits depends in large part upon how well the problem-solving requirements of your work match your preferred style or blend of styles.

Style of Problem Solving
Originality and Invention (introducing the new, different, or unique into being)
- Inventing ▪ creating ▪ originating ▪ designing
- coining ▪ conceiving ▪ authoring ▪ innovating
- giving birth to a new idea ▪ being resourceful . . .

Development and Extension (improving upon what exists)

■ Adapting ■ refining ■ making better ■ improving upon ■ advancing ■ perfecting ■ honing ■ modifying ■ correcting ■ changing ■ clarifying ■ sharpening ■ enhancing ■ remodeling ■ overhauling ■ strengthening ■ adjusting . . .

Reproduction and Maintenance (implementing past, proven solutions)

■ Standardizing ■ troubleshooting ■ conforming ■ duplicating ■ maintaining continuity ■ sustaining sameness ■ perpetuating uniformity ■ following set patterns and procedures . . .

Providing Structure

Every one of us, whatever our background or upbringing, has a built-in predisposition toward arranging our lives along certain lines, a way of ordering the details of our world. As I mentioned earlier, you and I are creatures of structure. We are individual reflections of the Original Organizer.

Within the first few chapters of Genesis we find God hard at it, categorizing His creation into varieties of vegetation, labeling the light "day" and the darkness "night," scheduling the seasons . . . in short, doing whatever was necessary to plan and organize the perfect environment for humans to inhabit.

Each of us has a particular style or blend of components that characterizes our preferred ways of bringing structure to the details of our world. Your preference for bringing structure to bear upon your world is an important variable in piecing together the pattern of your best functioning in the world of work.

Mike is a goal-setter. Setting and aiming for predetermined objectives has always been a strong pattern in his enjoyable accomplishments. When he was on a trip with his folks at age twelve, he set a goal of jumping off the diving board at the motel pool one hundred times. At fifteen he decided to learn in one week how to juggle three balls. As a sales representative for his company, Mike sets for himself a virtual smorgasbord of goals ranging from daily do-lists to year-end sales objectives. Setting a continual array of goals is the way Mike brings order to his world and structure to his life.

Linda likes to proceduralize things. When she was a teenager she made a list outlining the steps she regularly took to clean her room and kept it on the wall above her desk. "I took great joy in putting on paper the steps it took to get various things done," she says. Today she writes "how-to" books for women about home and car maintenance, fully utilizing and thoroughly enjoying the investment of this element of her Functional Design.

Robert, Margaret, and William publish a popular, industry-related newsletter. "We love working together because each of us enjoys our role and function," they say. As a committee of three they decide on themes for each month of the coming year. Then they divide and conquer.

Robert categorizes and keeps track of various story ideas and data that all three of them come across. Each month Margaret culls through Robert's well-ordered data bank for all the stories related to the current theme. She prioritizes them according to their perceived value, selects the top three, and edits their wording and style. The baton is then passed to William, who takes the prepared material and structures it into a nicely formatted and packaged finished product, ready to be reproduced and mailed. All three of them know their own best style of structuring their world, and they offer it through their work to help achieve the goals of the team.

Style of Providing Structure
- Budgeting
- Building
- Categorizing

- Collecting
- Detailing
- Diagramming
- Goal-setting
- Integrating
- Master-planning
- Packaging
- Proceduralizing
- Programming
- Synthesizing
- Other . . .

People Influencing

"In the beginning was the Word," begins John's Gospel, "and the Word was with God, and the Word was God." When we speak of God we must first recognize that He communicates; He is always moving toward us. His "people influencing" originates in a loving heart, which communicates that love through word and act.

As individuals made in God's image, we have been designed as agents of influence — instruments of impact on our world. We can understand the nature of this influence from two perspectives: (1) the *function* it serves, and (2) the *form* it takes. So now we'll look at the "what" and the "how" of the ways in which we influence others.

1. The function of our influence. The following categories represent the various functions of influence I've discovered in the people I've studied. Most people display a blend of two or at most three — with one style tending to predominate. For example, a "craftsman-specialist" might primarily gravitate toward focusing on research projects, yet also enjoy sharing his expertise with others in a "counselor-consultant" role. I've categorized these functions in seven areas:

■ "Director-manager." Prefers a role in which she determines direction, then works through the efforts of others to move in that direction. Key functions include taking charge, giving direction, controlling the action of others toward objectives.

■ "Coordinator-facilitator." Prefers a role in which he provides organization and resources to help people reach their commonly held objectives. His key functions include helping to clarify common objectives, incorporating individual contributions into blended effort, providing resources and information to enable coordinated effort toward objectives.

■ "Promoter-advocate." This person gravitates toward the role of a cheerleader of direction and objectives. Unlike the director-manager, she prefers to work only on people, not through them. Her strengths lie in motivating, stimulating, recruiting, selling, sponsoring, championing, convincing, politicking.

■ "Frontrunner-pacesetter." Prefers a role in which he sets a personal example, a model of behavior for others to follow. He likes to live out in front, showing the way by action.

■ "Teacher-coach." She prefers a role in which she cultivates the knowledge and talents of others. You'll find her at her best while instructing, training, developing, and equipping other people around her.

■ "Counselor-consultant." This person is most comfortable in roles in which the focus is on providing a specialized information service to directly aid and assist others. He is best at advising, informing, recommending, and enabling others concerning his area of expertise.

■ "Craftsman-specialist." She desires a role in which her focus is on the information and techniques of her own contribution. People are only indirectly involved as beneficiaries of her contribution. Her key functions include performing a task or producing a product and contributing it as her part of the whole.

The key to unlocking the real truth of your design in this realm lies not in what you're thinking to yourself as you've read through these descriptions. Depending on your mood and how things are going today, you might see yourself as all of the above, or none of the above. That's why I believe that checklists as a primary method of self-assessment are too subjective.

For many years I viewed myself as a teacher. Only upon careful and honest assessment of my enjoyable accomplishments did I realize that I'm not really a teacher—at least not in a primary sense. I'm a blend of craftsman-specialist, counselor-consultant, and promoter-advocate who had filled the role of a teacher—even though I really had products and expertise and promotional influence more on my mind than the development of people. Without careful assessment of the broader scope of my life through studying the various elements of my enjoyable accomplishments, I would have clung to an incomplete, poorly focused idea of what I really wanted to do.

So the real key is the data you've provided on yourself in the last chapter. Here the consistent patterns emerge. In chapter 7 I'll ask you to look back through these pictures of your past to find the *real* story of how you influence others when you are involved in your enjoyable work.

2. The form of our influence. I once interviewed a very unique client who thoroughly enjoyed expressing his emotions through his arms and hands. His preferred form of influence, in other words, had a great deal to do with body language. Not surprisingly, he's always enjoyed acting and being in school plays. Today he's an aspiring young thespian. Perhaps one day I'll see him in the movies!

Another client spent many hours of her youth writing letters to friends and writing down her thoughts about life in notebooks. Obviously, her preferred form of influence focused on use of the written word. Today she is a research assistant for the author of many books.

Yet another friend gravitates toward verbal interaction with others. In high school he loved debating issues in social studies class. His greatest joy came from open-forum discussions with classmates concerning books they read for their political science class. Today he's pursuing a degree as a teacher. "I know that what I want to do most in life is to interact with people, getting them to think and then verbalize their thoughts."

Recently I spent some time with an individual whose main form of people influence could be characterized as creating environments. She thoroughly enjoys opening up her home to people, influencing them in an atmosphere uniquely her own.

The form of your people-influencing style is only one element within the whole picture of your Functional Design, but it is an important one. Identifying and living within the boundaries of your preferred functions and forms of influencing others can be a liberating experience.

Understanding this element of my own Functional Design helped relieve the frustration I experienced as a campus minister, in which I was asked to deal with a wide spectrum of issues and problems. As I began to realize my need for focus and specialization, and as I began to accept and live within my God-designed boundaries of influence, I became energized and more effective in doing the type of technical, consultative, and promotional work for which I was intended. It was like being set free from prison—Dave Frähm, released to make his best contribution to God's world. It demanded a career shift—something not easily accomplished, but made easier by my newfound commitment to the stewardship of my true talents.

As I studied my preferred style of people influencing, I realized that the form of influence I most enjoy is written correspondence. I'm one of those rare types who thoroughly enjoys writing and responding to letters. Each day, no matter what I'm doing, I find myself asking the question, "Now how would I put that into a newsletter?" Today it all fits very nicely into the consulting work and correspondence I do focused around the concepts of individual uniqueness and career direction.

Style of People Influencing
Function
- Director-manager
- Coordinator-facilitator
- Promoter-advocate
- Frontrunner-pacesetter
- Teacher-coach
- Counselor-consultant
- Craftsman-specialist

Form
- Verbal
- Written
- Visual
- Environmental

How about you? Can you identify your style of people influencing?

Don't be taken in by the ever popular C.A.N. — "corporate-America-nonsense" — principle, which measures success according to the highest rung you've reached in the climb to become top dog. If being in charge is indeed your function of influence, great! Climb the ladder until you reach your niche, doing so with humility and a sense of stewardship, watching out for the fingers of those around you.

There is no hierarchy of value in one function of influence over another, no better form than another. All are equally important: each has a blend of functions to fulfill and contributions to make. Each working context and its objectives define the styles needed, the leadership required.

Don't force yourself in where you don't fit. Apply your energies and talents where they're needed. Be what you are; understand where you fit. Make your best contribution, and you will be free to live the poem written just for *you* by the Master Poet.

CHAPTER SIX

PREFERRED INVESTMENTS
A Look into Your Portfolio

Lamech married two wives—Adah and Zillah. To Adah was
born a baby named Jabal. He became the first of the cattlemen
and those living in tents. His brother's name was Jubal,
the first musician—the inventor of the harp and flute. To
Lamech's other wife, Zillah, was born Tubal-Cain. He opened
the first foundry, forging instruments of bronze and iron.

Genesis 5:19-22 (TLB)

"Words are my life," said a journalist in a story she was
writing about her work. "Forming words into sentences and
phrases and paragraphs so that they say just what I want—
I've always enjoyed that. I like writing things that get attention, that move people to action, that stimulate them in some
new way."

Dusty boxes piled high in her cluttered attic contain the
treasures of a youth filled with writing poetry and short stories. In her adult years, she applies her gift with words as a
public relations journalist and liaison between the company
she works for and the community in which it's located.

"I used to work from my home as a freelance writer for
magazines and various news services, but I've come to realize that I work better when I'm surrounded by a team of
others who are doing the same thing," she reflected. "We

don't always work together on the same projects, but our goals are the same, and there is an aura of camaraderie that keeps me motivated. It's like we stimulate each other toward our best work just by being close by."

If you look with a trained eye at this woman's testimonial about her work, you'll find that the information she gave about herself falls into three categories. First, there are the *elements* with which she enjoys functioning—in this case, words. Second, she describes the *environment* that brings out her best—working in the midst of a group, yet responsible for her own project. And finally, she reveals the *ends* or results she enjoys accomplishing. She wants to move people with the words she writes.

To summarize this woman's preferences, we could say that she enjoys working with words, in a group setting, on individualized projects, to create written products that influence people. Of course, there is a great deal more to this woman than we can see in the few lines of her story above. But even with just this little bit of information we've already begun to identify some very powerful facts about her vocational identity.

It is this trilogy of elements, environments, and ends that forms what I refer to as your "preferred investments." This blend of information about you gives movement to the styles I introduced you to in the last chapter. If preferred styles are the chassis of a car, preferred investments are its motor.

In this chapter we're going to look at what makes you go. In every story, every Action Shot of your past accomplishments, you will find details of your preferred investment portfolio—oh yes, you've got one. It's discovered with ease—or should I say, "Es"!

ELEMENTS

King David looked out one day through his palace window across the plains of Israel and observed, "The earth is the

LORD's, and everything in it, the world, and all who live in it; for he founded it upon the seas and established it upon the waters" (Psalm 24:1-2).

God works with all the elements of His world. This is an important fact to grasp. Throughout the pages of Scripture, God reveals Himself in a wide array of capacities and roles—from master gardener and carpenter to teacher and priest. He is at home in all of them.

This truth gives us the freedom to explore where we best fit, as His stewards and co-creators. When God created each of us He designed us with a built-in preference for the way we function best. Given a choice, we will gravitate toward particular elements that attract our attention and energize us.

Let's look at a few chapters of Genesis to illustrate the point. Abel worked with flocks; Cain worked with dirt (4:2). Why did they pick different elements to work with? Tubal-Cain enjoyed forging hand tools out of bronze and iron. His half-brother enjoyed playing musical instruments as his vocational choice (4:21-22). A fellow named Nimrod took up the tools of a hunter (10:8-9). Ishmael made a career with bow and arrow (21:20).

Is it probable that these people had some overbearing teacher or pushy parent behind the scenes, telling them what to become? "Now son, I know you're thinking about becoming a chariot salesman like your Uncle Rubin, God rest his soul. But I think you should know—the big bucks are in the tool and die business!" I don't think so. God designed those individuals to move toward certain elements that caught their interest, just like He designs individual personalities today.

Clearly identifying the elements you prefer to function with is very important in the process of finding your place in the world of work. In the next chapter I'll help you select the elements with which you best function. But for now, look over this list of conventional elements you are likely to be involved with. The Great Niche Hunt assessment process groups elements into these "worlds":

Elements
- The world of animals
- The world of data
- The world of equipment
- The world of human behavior
- The world of the human body
- The world of logistics
- The world of machines (industrial)
- The world of machines (office)
- The world of manmade materials
- The world of math
- The world of money
- The world of natural resources
- The world of people
- The world of plants
- The world of sound
- The world of thought
- The world of vehicles
- The world of visuals
- The world of words

From childhood on, Jack was interested in the sciences. In junior high school he performed an experiment with his first chemistry set that nearly burned down the family garage. In high school he worked summers in a meat-packing plant. His coworkers thought him a bit "off-center" as he spent many a fascinated lunch hour musing over the muscle structure of cow carcasses.

When I met Jack he was a doctor in family practice medicine. He was spending a great deal of his time counseling patients about their health care program and being frustrated. It didn't take long for me to recognize from his enjoyable accomplishments that what he really liked most about medicine had more to do with data and the human body then it did with people relationships. The problem was that people relationships and human bodies tend to come in a package deal!

Jack left family practice and today specializes in medical research. As a Christian he had at first struggled with the feeling that perhaps he was running away from relating to people. I assured him that he was simply finding that place in the realm of things in which he could give his best *for* people, even if not directly *with* them.

Jack's relationships could come from friends and family and neighbors; but vocationally, he was much more suited to the realm of research. Paradoxically, Jack's general relationships with people were improved by his change to research rather than front-line work with patients. A better job fit brought with it much of the joy and freedom in Christ that Jack had been missing, and his life became far more attractive to others as a result.

ENVIRONMENT

Each of us has an environment, a set of surroundings that stimulates an inner sense of motivation and the energy to bring forth our best efforts.

I have noticed, for instance, that I'm at my best when left alone to focus complete attention on the task at hand. My wife, on the other hand, enjoys the camaraderie of others when she's working. To preserve harmony in our married life we've learned the fine, sometimes tricky, art of adjusting to each other's environmental preferences. And yet the importance of our individual uniquenesses in this area has not been lost on our work lives. We do all we can to incorporate these energizing factors into our work environments beyond home and marriage.

Just as a horse has an appetite that keeps him moving forward to get the carrot dangling in front of him, you and I have been designed with a blend of individual "appetites"—environmental factors—that keep us moving forward and energized in our world and work.

Why does the professional mountain climber labor up the mountain? "Because it's there!" is the classic answer. The mountain challenges his physical abilities with a risk that stimulates his spirit of adventure. But ask a sane person about mountain climbing—me, for instance—and he'll tell you a different story. The environmental factors that pump excitement and energy into the veins of my climbing friends and make them willing to risk life and limb leave me comatose. Give me a word processor and call on me to use my intellectual abilities to write stories about life, and—wow!—I'm on top of the world.

Let's look at three categories of environmental factors that play a very significant role in career development, job selection, and job satisfaction:

■ Preferred supervision.
■ Preferred teamwork.
■ Preferred conditions.

In the next chapter you will have the opportunity to chart out those aspects of your environment that reveal themselves as important to your own best efforts. Now, look through the following list describing various aspects of the work environment:

Environments
Preferred Supervision
■ None
■ Sponsorship
■ Delegation
■ Directive

Preferred Teamwork
■ Group effort
■ Individualized effort in a group context
■ Independent effort

Preferred Conditions
- Academic ■ aesthetic ■ cause ■ challenge
- competition ■ conformity ■ conservatism
- creativity ■ deficiency ■ discipline ■ efficiency
- flexibility ■ orderly ■ physical ■ practical
- predictability ■ precision ■ pressure ■ repetition
- risk ■ rules ■ spontaneity ■ travel ■ other . . .

Bill, the former frozen yogurt entrepreneur, develops his expertise presenting seminars for the consulting company that employs him. From an environmental point of view, the following factors seem to bring out his best: directive supervision, individualized effort within a group context, and the conditions of conformity, predictability, repetition, and requirements.

As you can see, Bill thrives in a rather rigid environment, which could make people with other preferences feel quite controlled and constrained. But as he tells it, "I love regimentation . . . regularity . . . following outlined procedures for everything."

Elizabeth, on the other hand, would wilt under such constraints. She enjoys going beyond the boundaries. Her preferred environment includes, among other things, these descriptors: a blend of either no supervision or sponsorship, independent effort, and creativity.

Important to your niche hunt is knowing the environmental factors that "turn you on," then maximizing the energy that results. Perhaps many of the people who would rather go back to bed in the morning than head off for their jobs are simply experiencing a "malnutrition" of environmental factors in their work—factors that are important to their emotional and functional well-being. As I mentioned earlier, people who work in jobs for long periods of time in such a deficit state wind up in emotional bankruptcy—or burnout.

As an aspect of personal stewardship, burned-out persons

must take personal responsibility for change, either by nego-tiating change in their current job or changing jobs alto-gether. Just taking a little time off from a job for which you're ill-suited is like putting a Band-Aid over skin cancer. Even though you can't see it at first, it's getting worse!

ENDS

"The LORD works out everything for his own ends," wrote King Solomon (Proverbs 16:4). Indeed, God is a purposeful Being. At the end of His every action there is a goal in mind, an intended result.

You and I, designed in His image, operate similarly. Each of us is predisposed to move toward certain outcomes through our actions. You've heard some people, perhaps yourself, tagged as being "goal-oriented." The news is that *all* of us are oriented toward achieving certain goals, which bring out our best efforts. Richard Bolles refers to them as your "favorite outcomes."

"We are talking about outcomes, or where does it all lead to?" writes Richard Bolles. "At the work I most love to do, what result am I aiming at? Do I want to help produce a product, or do I want to help offer some service to people, or do I want to help gather, manage, or disseminate infor-mation to people? Or all three? Or two? And in what order of priority?"[1]

Preferred Results

For purposes of the Great Niche Hunt, I've adapted and modified these three categories into the following: (1) making things, (2) meeting needs, and (3) moving people. I call them the "3 Ms" of preferred results.

■ "Making things" means that your activity is aimed primarily at bringing forth some product, goods, produce, handiwork, creation, performance, show, presentation, and so on.

■ "Meeting needs" means that you enjoy helping to provide the necessary information, resources, or knowhow to solve problems and address concerns people might have.

■ "Moving people" means that you enjoy making a contribution aimed primarily at impacting and influencing the thoughts and behavior of others.

Let's look at a few examples.

My wife is an artist. Now when I say "artist," most people think of someone sitting for hours in front of a canvas producing a beautiful work of art. Anne is wonderfully gifted at this, but she does not gravitate primarily toward making things. Her preferred result is primarily meeting needs; only secondarily, making things.

Before we had clearly identified this element of Anne's Functional Design, she had begun a small business venture of designing and producing her own line of greeting cards. But the primary focus of making things soon left her emotionally uninvolved. We examined the issue of her preferred results and came up with a plan for her to meet needs by providing an interior decorating consultant service. For her it's a wonderful way of using her artistic gifts in a needs-meeting venture. She still produces an array of things such as designs and floor plans—but she does so primarily in response to customer requests for assistance.

My friend William has always enjoyed a blend of preferred results that includes moving people and making things, in that order of priority. Everything he's ever enjoyed doing revolves around the theme of influencing people—recruiting them to activities, stimulating them toward new thinking, selling them on an idea. But along with that, he inevitably likes to include the production of some product that would enhance the recruitment, the stimulation, and the sales pitch.

Today, William is employed by a large hotel chain. He calls on potential clients to solicit their future business. In the process he's developed his own set of sales tools and products—brochures, overheads, and slide shows.

And then there's Jack, the family practice doctor turned researcher. He realized that what he really wanted to do in the field of medicine had more to do with helping to make things—medical products—than it did with meeting needs or moving people.

Preferred Rewards

Side by side with our preferred *results* is the category of preferred *rewards*. This is the second element that defines the ends we move toward. Rewards are what motivate us to produce results; they are the longings we seek to fulfill through our actions in this world. Mattson and Miller refer to "central motivated thrusts."[2] Frederick Herzberg labels them "motivators."[3] Whatever the titles, we all have them. As King Solomon pointed out: "Hope deferred makes the heart sick, but a longing fulfilled is a tree of life" (Proverbs 13:12).

These universal longings take particular form within each of us. The rewards that I seek from my own involvement in the world of work are not necessarily the same rewards that you seek. Nor are yours quite like those of another. And while some rewards can only be given by another (extrinsic), others are satisfied internally by the things we're able to accomplish (intrinsic). The following list should help you understand these categories:

Ends

Preferred Results
- Making things
- Meeting needs
- Moving people

Preferred Rewards
Intrinsic
- Being creative ■ being unique, different ■ gaining mastery, expertise ■ producing quality, excellence

---

■ winning, beating the competition ■ overcoming obstacles, challenges ■ reaching goals, accomplishing objectives ■ learning new things ■ keeping things organized, under control ■ fulfilling requirements ■ making progress ■ acquiring what's needed ■ communicating, being self-expressive ■ excelling, being the best ■ maximizing potential ■ solving problems, making things work ■ making an impact ■ other . . .

Extrinsic
■ Money ■ recognition ■ respect ■ reputation ■ opportunity ■ inclusion ■ response ■ responsibility ■ authority ■ freedom ■ justice ■ other . . .

Elizabeth has always been motivated by catalyzing a response in others—an extrinsic reward. She loves to get people to laugh or cheer or applaud. In the world of stage and performance, such rewards have been lavished upon her. But in the world of selling insurance, which currently taps most of her time and energy, her reward system is left noticeably unfulfilled. "I'm making a decent living," Elizabeth comments, "but the response I'm getting from potential clients is more often than not the wrong one." For her, audience response ranks higher in importance than money as a reward in her work.

One of the strongest elements within George's reward system is gaining expertise—an intrinsic reward. He has always loved figuring out how certain machines worked, what made them go, what they could accomplish. In school he discovered how a certain piece of technology could perform functions that even its inventors were unaware of. "To me it's extremely rewarding just to know that I've mastered the thing," he says.

In the world of work the reward system of each individual plays a very significant part in job satisfaction and stewardship. Generally speaking, the most common rewards are either more money or new responsibilities—which aren't enough to keep some people going.

I read an article written by a man who left a decent-paying job in search of more independence to be creative. His employer had offered him a very attractive pay raise, but "what I really wanted," he says, "was more freedom of expression, not more money. I've never really considered the amount of money I earn to be as important as my freedom to be creative. And since the company hasn't given me the freedom, I'm leaving." He took a fifty percent cut in earnings to fulfill his own longing for a different sort of reward. He now co-owns and operates a custom wallpaper designing business with his wife.

The teacher who excels at teaching because she loves it, and who finds reward in getting her students to respond to the subject matter, is in great danger of being "vocationally abused" if someone boots her up the proverbial ladder to an administration job. Instead of gaining a gifted administrator, the world has just lost a gifted teacher. Such things happen all the time because of a general ignorance of individualized reward systems.

In chapter 7 you'll be able to take some time to analyze *your* system of rewards as you follow your tracks back through your Action Shots of enjoyable accomplishments. I'll also help you identify your blend of preferred results in priority order. Together we'll explore how you can manage your own portfolio to maximize the investments you've been designed to make in your world of work.

CHAPTER SEVEN

WHAT COLOR IS YOUR PAIR OF SHOES?

Discovering the "Real You" in Your Past

> There is a real sense of freedom associated with understanding how God has "wired" us. It is really liberating to be able to say, "I can do that, but it really wouldn't be my best contribution. This is the way I can be a resource and best serve both the Lord's and your interests."
>
> **Bruce Kittleson**, a friend of mine

Do you remember from your childhood that wonderful story *The Wizard of Oz*? A cyclone carries farm girl Dorothy from Kansas to a strange and wondrous new world, the Land of Oz.

But Dorothy isn't in Oz long before she wants to go home, where she belongs. But Kansas—wherever it is now—is surely a long way from the Land of Oz.

After Dorothy has wrung her hands for the tenth time and buried her tear-streaked face in her dog Toto's fur, she comes to a rather startling realization: All along the very thing she needs to find her way back home has been right beneath her feet. Her ruby-red slippers are the key to getting back to Kansas. Just grab the dog, click those heels together, and poof!—she's home free.

Do you see the connection? You and I hold within ourselves

some very important pieces to the puzzle of finding the place where we fit in the world of work. Those pieces form what I've been referring to as your Functional Design, the motivational threads hidden in the stories of your past enjoyable accomplishments. Like Dorothy, you need to understand what you already have—the "shoes" you've been walking around in all your life that appear too ordinary and obvious to be significant.

You're going to be spending a lot of time looking back through the Action Shots you wrote out in chapter 4. In order to avoid flipping back and forth as you work through the assessment charts in this chapter, you might want to stop and make photocopies of your Action Shots so you can have them at your fingertips.

Before you go any farther, *if you haven't finished writing out your Action Shots in detail, please go back and do so now.* These written stories form the data bank containing the information you will need to fill out the following charts. This data bank reveals you in your past. Without this recorded data to draw from, the process of checking off items in the assessment charts will be quite subjective—varying with how you may be feeling or thinking at the moment.

Once your Action Shots are complete, the assigned number from one to seven will correspond to the numbered boxes that follow.

And now roll up your sleeves, get out your pencil, and prepare to discover the "real you" reflected in your past. This chapter will help you find the place where you belong. So click your heels together—you're almost home!

OVERVIEW

It's quite possible that all the information of chapters 5 and 6 has become somewhat jumbled together in your mind—as if you've dumped the contents of a 1000-piece puzzle out on the table and now have to figure out the patterns.

The following summary provides an overview of the

elements we've looked at in detail in the last two chapters. This outline provides the framework within which you will fit the pieces of your Functional Design. Each of the charts that follow covers one section of this outline.

Functional Design Overview
Preferred Styles
- Style of Processing Information
  Perception
  Judgment
- Style of Problem Solving
- Style of Producing Structure
- Style of People Influencing
  Function
  Form

Preferred Investments
- Elements
- Environments
  Preferred Supervision
  Preferred Teamwork
  Preferred Conditions
- Ends
  Results
  Rewards

Here are two keys to unlocking the value of the following charts:

- Consider them as guides, not masters. Feel free to be expansive, to add to each chart the terms that might better capture the essence of your patterns. The task is to accurately describe yourself in terms you understand.
- Look for patterns, recurrences. At the same time, realize that not every Action Shot will give relevant data for each chart.

PREFERRED STYLES

Style of Processing Information—Perception
(how you prefer to gain an awareness of your world)

For each of your seven Action Shots, go down this list of styles in which we gain awareness of our world. Put a "✔" in the appropriate boxes that describe how you gained awareness about your world as revealed by that particular Action Shot. Circle descriptors that serve to clarify, adding others that you find recurring in your data.

Interacting/Discussing

Listening to and sharing ideas with others, exchanging views, engaging in dialogue, conferring, comparing notes, talking things through, brainstorming ideas with others, discussing possibilities . . .

❑ 1 ❑ 2 ❑ 3 ❑ 4 ❑ 5 ❑ 6 ❑ 7

Observing/Listening

Watching, seeing, noticing, viewing, on the scene exposure to, listening in on, picking up subtle clues . . .

❑ 1 ❑ 2 ❑ 3 ❑ 4 ❑ 5 ❑ 6 ❑ 7

Doing/Trying

Hands-on experience, experimenting, trial and error, testing out, seeing what works, learning while you go, self-discovery . . .

❑ 1 ❑ 2 ❑ 3 ❑ 4 ❑ 5 ❑ 6 ❑ 7

Fact Finding/Data Collecting

Reading, studying, conducting surveys, asking questions, interviewing, researching the data, investigating . . .

❑ 1 ❑ 2 ❑ 3 ❑ 4 ❑ 5 ❑ 6 ❑ 7

Imagining/Envisioning

Visualizing, picturing, mental imaging, conceptualizing . . .

❑ 1 ❑ 2 ❑ 3 ❑ 4 ❑ 5 ❑ 6 ❑ 7

Summary—Style of Processing Information, Perception:
My two or three most recurrent ways of gaining an awareness about my world are . . .

(Styles)   (Descriptors)

_____   _____

                           _____

_____   _____

                           _____

_____   _____

                           _____

Style of Processing Information—Judgment
(how you prefer to draw conclusions about your world)

Put a "✔" in the appropriate boxes that describe how you drew conclusions about your world in your seven Action Shots. Circle descriptors that further clarify your style, adding any others that you find recurring in your data.

Analyzing (focusing on parts and their relationships)

Identifying common threads, determining patterns, seeing the steps involved, verifying ingredients, isolating the various factors to be considered, correlating, making distinctions between, dissecting, identifying contrasts or similarities . . .

❏ 1　❏ 2　❏ 3　❏ 4　❏ 5　❏ 6　❏ 7

Evaluating (focusing on value, potential, possibilities)

Assessing, appraising, pricing, reviewing, critiquing, judging the merits of, sizing up, grading, scoring, weighing options, measuring against a standard, comparing to a model or ideal, rating, weighing pros and cons . . .

❏ 1　❏ 2　❏ 3　❏ 4　❏ 5　❏ 6　❏ 7

Interpreting (focusing on meaning, intent, implication)

Explaining, clarifying, defining, translating, diagnosing, deducing, construing, inferring, reading into, identifying implications, reading between the lines, having a sense of rightness about . . .

❏ 1　❏ 2　❏ 3　❏ 4　❏ 5　❏ 6　❏ 7

Other:

❑ 1   ❑ 2   ❑ 3   ❑ 4   ❑ 5   ❑ 6   ❑ 7

Summary—Style of Processing Information, Judgment:
My two or three most recurrent ways of drawing conclusions about my world are . . .

(Styles)   (Descriptors)

_____   _____

                          _____

_____   _____

                          _____

_____   _____

                          _____

Style of Problem Solving
Again put a "✔" in each appropriate box that describes the
style of problem solving you used in each of your seven Action
Shots. Circle the descriptors that apply to your story, adding
others that you find recurring in your data.

Originality and Invention
(introducing the new, different, or unique into being)
Inventing, creating, originating, designing, coining, conceiving, authoring, innovating . . .
      ❏ 1 ❏ 2 ❏ 3 ❏ 4 ❏ 5 ❏ 6 ❏ 7

Development and Extension
(improving the potential and possibilities of what
exists)
Adapting, refining, maximizing, making better, improving
upon, advancing, perfecting, honing, modifying, correcting,
blending, clarifying, sharpening, enhancing . . .
      ❏ 1 ❏ 2 ❏ 3 ❏ 4 ❏ 5 ❏ 6 ❏ 7

Reproduction and Maintenance
(implementing past, proven solutions)
Standardizing, troubleshooting, conforming, duplicating,
maintaining continuity, sustaining sameness, following set
patterns and procedures, perpetuating uniformity, following a blueprint . . .
      ❏ 1 ❏ 2 ❏ 3 ❏ 4 ❏ 5 ❏ 6 ❏ 7

Summary—Style of Problem Solving:

My primary style of
problem solving is . . .   (Descriptors)

_____   _____

_____

_____

My secondary style of
problem solving is . . .

_____   _____

_____

_____

Style of Producing Structure

Check the appropriate boxes for the ways in which you brought order and structure to your world. Circle clarifying words, adding additional ones that you find in your seven Action Shots.

Budgeting
Allocating, allotting, rationing . . .
    ❑ 1 ❑ 2 ❑ 3 ❑ 4 ❑ 5 ❑ 6 ❑ 7

Building
Assembling, constructing, putting together . . .
    ❑ 1 ❑ 2 ❑ 3 ❑ 4 ❑ 5 ❑ 6 ❑ 7

Categorizing
Grouping, arranging, classifying, prioritizing, positioning . . .
    ❑ 1 ❑ 2 ❑ 3 ❑ 4 ❑ 5 ❑ 6 ❑ 7

Collecting
Accumulating, acquiring, amassing, compiling, gathering together . . .
    ❑ 1 ❑ 2 ❑ 3 ❑ 4 ❑ 5 ❑ 6 ❑ 7

Detailing
Dealing with specifics, particulars, the "nitty gritty" . . .
    ❑ 1 ❑ 2 ❑ 3 ❑ 4 ❑ 5 ❑ 6 ❑ 7

Diagramming
Charting, illustrating, drawing out, blueprinting . . .
    ❑ 1 ❑ 2 ❑ 3 ❑ 4 ❑ 5 ❑ 6 ❑ 7

Goal-Setting
Plotting direction, determining aim, setting objectives, targeting . . .
    ❑ 1 ❑ 2 ❑ 3 ❑ 4 ❑ 5 ❑ 6 ❑ 7

Integrating
Unifying, putting together into a whole, combining, incorporating . . .

❑ 1　❑ 2　❑ 3　❑ 4　❑ 5　❑ 6　❑ 7

Master-Planning
Determining overall strategy, putting forth a vision, "developing the big picture" . . .

❑ 1　❑ 2　❑ 3　❑ 4　❑ 5　❑ 6　❑ 7

Packaging
Putting into pass-on-able form, formatting . . .

❑ 1　❑ 2　❑ 3　❑ 4　❑ 5　❑ 6　❑ 7

Proceduralizing
Setting guidelines, determining policies, identifying standard operating procedures, systematizing, establishing methods . . .

❑ 1　❑ 2　❑ 3　❑ 4　❑ 5　❑ 6　❑ 7

Programming
Imposing a sequence of events, scheduling, setting agendas, planning meetings, creating frameworks . . .

❑ 1　❑ 2　❑ 3　❑ 4　❑ 5　❑ 6　❑ 7

Synthesizing
Reducing, condensing, compacting, abbreviating, consolidating, summarizing . . .

❑ 1　❑ 2　❑ 3　❑ 4　❑ 5　❑ 6　❑ 7

Other:

❑ 1　❑ 2　❑ 3　❑ 4　❑ 5　❑ 6　❑ 7

Summary—Style of Producing Structure:
My two to four most recurrent ways of bringing structure to my world include . . .

(Styles)   (Descriptors)

_____   _____

                            _____

_____   _____

                            _____

_____   _____

                            _____

_____   _____

                            _____

Style of People Influencing—Function
Check the boxes that describe the style of influence you had
on people in each of your Action Shots.

Director-Manager
(like a traffic cop outside a football stadium)
Prefers to determine direction, then control the action of
others to move in that direction . . .
      ❑ 1 ❑ 2 ❑ 3 ❑ 4 ❑ 5 ❑ 6 ❑ 7

Taking charge, giving direction, controlling the action of
others toward objectives . . .
      ❑ 1 ❑ 2 ❑ 3 ❑ 4 ❑ 5 ❑ 6 ❑ 7

Coordinator-Facilitator
(like the band leader at a football game)
Prefers to provide organization and resources in ways that
help people reach their commonly held objectives . . .
      ❑ 1 ❑ 2 ❑ 3 ❑ 4 ❑ 5 ❑ 6 ❑ 7

Helps to clarify common objectives, incorporate individual contribution into blended effort, provide resources
and/or information to enable coordinated effort toward
objectives . . .
      ❑ 1 ❑ 2 ❑ 3 ❑ 4 ❑ 5 ❑ 6 ❑ 7

Frontrunner-Pacesetter
(like a player/captain of a football team)
Prefers to set a personal example for others to follow . . .
      ❑ 1 ❑ 2 ❑ 3 ❑ 4 ❑ 5 ❑ 6 ❑ 7

Trend-setting, showing the way by example, modeling, "out
in front," "leading the charge" . . .
      ❑ 1 ❑ 2 ❑ 3 ❑ 4 ❑ 5 ❑ 6 ❑ 7

Promoter-Advocate
(like a fan at a football game)

Prefers taking a role as "cheerleader" of direction and objectives . . .

❑ 1   ❑ 2   ❑ 3   ❑ 4   ❑ 5   ❑ 6   ❑ 7

Motivating, stimulating, recruiting, sponsoring, championing, inspiring . . .

❑ 1   ❑ 2   ❑ 3   ❑ 4   ❑ 5   ❑ 6   ❑ 7

Teacher-Coach
(like the coach of a football team)

Prefers to cultivate knowledge and talents of others . . .

❑ 1   ❑ 2   ❑ 3   ❑ 4   ❑ 5   ❑ 6   ❑ 7

Instructing, training, developing, equipping, preparing, mentoring . . .

❑ 1   ❑ 2   ❑ 3   ❑ 4   ❑ 5   ❑ 6   ❑ 7

Counselor-Consultant
(like the team doctor for a football team)

Prefers to focus on providing specialized information services . . .

❑ 1   ❑ 2   ❑ 3   ❑ 4   ❑ 5   ❑ 6   ❑ 7

Informing, advising, recommending, prescribing, functioning as a resource, sharing expertise . . .

❑ 1   ❑ 2   ❑ 3   ❑ 4   ❑ 5   ❑ 6   ❑ 7

Craftsman-Specialist
(like the groundskeeper at a football stadium)

Prefers to focus on information and techniques of personal contribution to the whole . . .

❑ 1   ❑ 2   ❑ 3   ❑ 4   ❑ 5   ❑ 6   ❑ 7

Performing a task, producing a product . . .

❑ 1   ❑ 2   ❑ 3   ❑ 4   ❑ 5   ❑ 6   ❑ 7

Summary—Style of People Influencing, Function:
The two or three most recurrent functions of my people influencing are . . .

_____

_____

_____

Style of People Influencing—Form
Check the boxes and circle the descriptors that describe the form in which you influenced people. Add additional descriptors as appropriate.

Verbal
Presentations, conversations, face-to-face interactions . . .
❏ 1 ❏ 2 ❏ 3 ❏ 4 ❏ 5 ❏ 6 ❏ 7

Written
Personal letters, newsletters, books, papers, memos . . .
❏ 1 ❏ 2 ❏ 3 ❏ 4 ❏ 5 ❏ 6 ❏ 7

Visual
Body language, photographs, drawings, graphics, charts, multi-media presentations, dancing, signaling, mime . . .
❏ 1 ❏ 2 ❏ 3 ❏ 4 ❏ 5 ❏ 6 ❏ 7

Environmental
Creating atmospheres, setting tones, building relation-ships, opening your home to others . . .
❏ 1 ❏ 2 ❏ 3 ❏ 4 ❏ 5 ❏ 6 ❏ 7

Other:

❏ 1 ❏ 2 ❏ 3 ❏ 4 ❏ 5 ❏ 6 ❏ 7

Summary—Style of People Influencing, Form:
The two or three most recurrent forms of my people influencing are . . .

(Styles)   (Descriptors)

_____   _____

                    _____

_____   _____

                    _____

_____   _____

                    _____

PREFERRED INVESTMENTS

Elements (with which you prefer to function in your enjoyable accomplishments)

Put a "✔" in the appropriate boxes that describe the worlds of elements with which you preferred to function in your seven Action Shots. Circle descriptors, making any additions to these lists that further identify the elements with which you enjoy functioning.

The World of Animals
Cattle, racing horses, house pets, show animals, fish, zoo animals . . .

❑ 1 ❑ 2 ❑ 3 ❑ 4 ❑ 5 ❑ 6 ❑ 7

The World of Data
Statistics, findings, facts, forecasts, predictions, estimates, figures, measurements, counts, calculations, budgets, accounts, numbers, reports, records, inventories, trends . . .

❑ 1 ❑ 2 ❑ 3 ❑ 4 ❑ 5 ❑ 6 ❑ 7

The World of Equipment
Hand tools, art supplies, kilns, camera equipment, sports equipment, sound equipment, exercise equipment, lawn care equipment . . .

❑ 1 ❑ 2 ❑ 3 ❑ 4 ❑ 5 ❑ 6 ❑ 7

The World of Human Behavior
Habits, traditions, customs, cultures, family systems, emotions, responses, temperaments, humor, personalities, character traits, mannerisms, strengths, talents, drives, motivations, gifts . . .

❑ 1 ❑ 2 ❑ 3 ❑ 4 ❑ 5 ❑ 6 ❑ 7

The World of the Human Body
Blood, skin, hair, bones and joints, eyesight, ears and hearing, teeth . . .

❏ 1   ❏ 2   ❏ 3   ❏ 4   ❏ 5   ❏ 6   ❏ 7

The World of Logistics
Plans, strategies, tactics, schedules, timetables, agendas, arrangements, methods, techniques, procedures, "how-to's" . . .

❏ 1   ❏ 2   ❏ 3   ❏ 4   ❏ 5   ❏ 6   ❏ 7

The World of Machines (industrial)
Manufacturing equipment, robots, printing press, drill press, metal stamp . . .

❏ 1   ❏ 2   ❏ 3   ❏ 4   ❏ 5   ❏ 6   ❏ 7

The World of Machines (office)
Copier, calculator, computer, telephone, answering machine, fax machine . . .

❏ 1   ❏ 2   ❏ 3   ❏ 4   ❏ 5   ❏ 6   ❏ 7

The World of Man-Made Materials
Paper, steel, glass, fabric, lumber, paint, foodstuff, chemicals, plastics, concrete . . .

❏ 1   ❏ 2   ❏ 3   ❏ 4   ❏ 5   ❏ 6   ❏ 7

The World of Math
Formulas, theorems, equations . . .

❏ 1   ❏ 2   ❏ 3   ❏ 4   ❏ 5   ❏ 6   ❏ 7

The World of Money
Investments, banking, accounting, bookkeeping, taxes, funds, interest rates . . .

❏ 1   ❏ 2   ❏ 3   ❏ 4   ❏ 5   ❏ 6   ❏ 7

The World of Natural Resources
Water, wind, air, solar power, electricity, soil, forests, rocks, minerals, weather . . .
❏ 1 ❏ 2 ❏ 3 ❏ 4 ❏ 5 ❏ 6 ❏ 7

The World of People
Clients, customers, audiences, employees, team members, trainees . . .
❏ 1 ❏ 2 ❏ 3 ❏ 4 ❏ 5 ❏ 6 ❏ 7

The World of Plants
House plants, farm crops, trees, flowers, shrubs, land-scaping . . .
❏ 1 ❏ 2 ❏ 3 ❏ 4 ❏ 5 ❏ 6 ❏ 7

The World of Sound
Music, special effects, recordings, acoustics, voice, rhythm, accents, singing, noise . . .
❏ 1 ❏ 2 ❏ 3 ❏ 4 ❏ 5 ❏ 6 ❏ 7

The World of Thought/Ideas
Beliefs, ideas, theories, concepts, philosophies, truths, morals, ethics, ideologies, religious convictions/systems, world views, values, doctrines, laws, principles, knowledge . . .
❏ 1 ❏ 2 ❏ 3 ❏ 4 ❏ 5 ❏ 6 ❏ 7

The World of Vehicles
Cars, planes, trains, boats, motorcycles, bicycles, forklifts, tractors, trailers, trucks . . .
❏ 1 ❏ 2 ❏ 3 ❏ 4 ❏ 5 ❏ 6 ❏ 7

The World of Visuals
Art forms, graphics, illustration, fashion, photos, videos, decorations, colors, architecture, blueprints, designs, layouts, drawings, cosmetics, home furnishings . . .
❏ 1 ❏ 2 ❏ 3 ❏ 4 ❏ 5 ❏ 6 ❏ 7

The World of Words

Language, literature, journalism, definitions, poetry, lyrics, mottos, jingles, quotes, stories . . .

❏ 1   ❏ 2   ❏ 3   ❏ 4   ❏ 5   ❏ 6   ❏ 7

Other:

❏ 1   ❏ 2   ❏ 3   ❏ 4   ❏ 5   ❏ 6   ❏ 7

Summary—Elements:
The four to six most recurrent "worlds" of elements with which I prefer to function are . . .

(Worlds)   (Descriptors)

_____   _____

                            _____

_____   _____

                            _____

_____   _____

                            _____

_____   _____

                            _____

_____   _____

                            _____

_____   _____

                            _____

**Environments (in which you prefer
to function)—Preferred Supervision**

Put a "✔" in the appropriate boxes that describe the type of
supervision you preferred in each of your Action Shots.

None

Operated independently from supervisory influence or control: self-determining, self-initiating, self-directing . . .
"Here's what I'm going to do."
 ❑ 1 ❑ 2 ❑ 3 ❑ 4 ❑ 5 ❑ 6 ❑ 7

Sponsorship

Was enabled and facilitated by supervisory authority in
making a self-initiated, self-directed contribution . . .
"Here's what I want to do; will you support me in it?"
 ❑ 1 ❑ 2 ❑ 3 ❑ 4 ❑ 5 ❑ 6 ❑ 7

Delegation

Was asked to take on certain assignments and given the
freedom to figure out how to accomplish them . . .
"Tell me what you'd like done and turn me loose."
 ❑ 1 ❑ 2 ❑ 3 ❑ 4 ❑ 5 ❑ 6 ❑ 7

Directive

Was given assignments with specific guidelines and requirements . . .
"Tell me what you want and how you want it."
 ❑ 1 ❑ 2 ❑ 3 ❑ 4 ❑ 5 ❑ 6 ❑ 7

Other:

 ❑ 1 ❑ 2 ❑ 3 ❑ 4 ❑ 5 ❑ 6 ❑ 7

Summary—Environments, Preferred Supervision:
The two most recurrent ways in which I prefer to be
supervised are . . .

(primary style) _____

(secondary style) _____

Environments—Preferred Teamwork

Check the appropriate boxes that describe the type of relationship you preferred with coworkers while accomplishing
the tasks in each of your seven Action Shots.

Group Effort

Preferred to accomplish tasks in a blended effort with
others . . .

    ❑ 1 ❑ 2 ❑ 3 ❑ 4 ❑ 5 ❑ 6 ❑ 7

Individualized Effort Within a Group Context

Preferred to accomplish personalized tasks within a group
context in which my efforts could be traced directly back to
me . . .

    ❑ 1 ❑ 2 ❑ 3 ❑ 4 ❑ 5 ❑ 6 ❑ 7

Independent Effort

Preferred to work alone in accomplishing the tasks
involved . . .

    ❑ 1 ❑ 2 ❑ 3 ❑ 4 ❑ 5 ❑ 6 ❑ 7

Summary—Environments, Preferred Teamwork:
My most recurrent style of teamworking with others
is . . .
_____

Environments—Preferred Conditions

Check the boxes that best describe the context and/or conditions in which your enjoyable accomplishments took place. Circle any descriptors that apply, and add your own.

Academic

Philosophical, conceptual, idea-oriented, cerebral, research and study, think tank, nurturing the mind . . .

❑ 1   ❑ 2   ❑ 3   ❑ 4   ❑ 5   ❑ 6   ❑ 7

Aesthetic

Beauty, artistic or literary, visual emphasis, nurturing the soul . . .

❑ 1   ❑ 2   ❑ 3   ❑ 4   ❑ 5   ❑ 6   ❑ 7

Cause

Mission, vision, campaign, quest, passion, "guiding light" . . .

❑ 1   ❑ 2   ❑ 3   ❑ 4   ❑ 5   ❑ 6   ❑ 7

Challenge

Problems, handicaps, obstacles, adversities, puzzles, tests, dilemmas, "hurdles to jump" . . .

❑ 1   ❑ 2   ❑ 3   ❑ 4   ❑ 5   ❑ 6   ❑ 7

Competition

Opposition, contests, rivalries, combat, "head-to-head encounters" . . .

❑ 1   ❑ 2   ❑ 3   ❑ 4   ❑ 5   ❑ 6   ❑ 7

Conformity
Uniformity, standardization, consistency, "straight and narrow" . . .

    ❏ 1 ❏ 2 ❏ 3 ❏ 4 ❏ 5 ❏ 6 ❏ 7

Conservatism
Safety, steady, unchanging, cautious, careful, traditional, conventional, orthodox, "tried and true," preserving the status quo . . .

    ❏ 1 ❏ 2 ❏ 3 ❏ 4 ❏ 5 ❏ 6 ❏ 7

Creativity
New, different, unique, imaginative, original, "marching to the beat of a different drum," "off the beaten path" . . .

    ❏ 1 ❏ 2 ❏ 3 ❏ 4 ❏ 5 ❏ 6 ❏ 7

Deficiency
Opportunity to correct inadequacies, weaknesses, insufficiencies, lacks, "needs to address" . . .

    ❏ 1 ❏ 2 ❏ 3 ❏ 4 ❏ 5 ❏ 6 ❏ 7

Discipline
Diligence, focused effort, comprehensiveness, thoroughness, "nose to the grindstone" . . .

    ❏ 1 ❏ 2 ❏ 3 ❏ 4 ❏ 5 ❏ 6 ❏ 7

Efficiency
Effective, productive, economic, thrifty, "a penny saved is a penny earned" . . .

    ❏ 1 ❏ 2 ❏ 3 ❏ 4 ❏ 5 ❏ 6 ❏ 7

Experimental
Exploratory, trying new things, "what if" . . .

    ❏ 1 ❏ 2 ❏ 3 ❏ 4 ❏ 5 ❏ 6 ❏ 7

Flexibility
Fluid, changing, responsive, "rolling with the punches" . . .
❏ 1 ❏ 2 ❏ 3 ❏ 4 ❏ 5 ❏ 6 ❏ 7

Orderly
Organized, structured, "ducks in a row," "a place for everything and everything in its place" . . .
❏ 1 ❏ 2 ❏ 3 ❏ 4 ❏ 5 ❏ 6 ❏ 7

Physical
Manual, athletic, "hands-on" . . .
❏ 1 ❏ 2 ❏ 3 ❏ 4 ❏ 5 ❏ 6 ❏ 7

Pioneer
Opening new territory, "breaking new ground" . . .
❏ 1 ❏ 2 ❏ 3 ❏ 4 ❏ 5 ❏ 6 ❏ 7

Practical
Useful, pragmatic, application-oriented, "down to earth," "nuts and bolts" . . .
❏ 1 ❏ 2 ❏ 3 ❏ 4 ❏ 5 ❏ 6 ❏ 7

Predictability
Stable, unchanging, consistent, "no surprises" . . .
❏ 1 ❏ 2 ❏ 3 ❏ 4 ❏ 5 ❏ 6 ❏ 7

Precision
Exactness, accuracy, preciseness, attention to detail, "to a T" . . .
❏ 1 ❏ 2 ❏ 3 ❏ 4 ❏ 5 ❏ 6 ❏ 7

Pressure
Stress, deadlines, "under the gun" . . .
❏ 1 ❏ 2 ❏ 3 ❏ 4 ❏ 5 ❏ 6 ❏ 7

Process
Ongoing, continuing, part of a larger whole, open-ended . . .
    ❑ 1 ❑ 2 ❑ 3 ❑ 4 ❑ 5 ❑ 6 ❑ 7

Projects
Tasks with a start and finish . . .
    ❑ 1 ❑ 2 ❑ 3 ❑ 4 ❑ 5 ❑ 6 ❑ 7

Repetition
Routine, methodical, systematic, habitual, regular, automatic, "like clockwork" . . .
    ❑ 1 ❑ 2 ❑ 3 ❑ 4 ❑ 5 ❑ 6 ❑ 7

Risk
Adventure, danger, excitement, uncertainty, chance, "out on a limb," "no guts, no glory" . . .
    ❑ 1 ❑ 2 ❑ 3 ❑ 4 ❑ 5 ❑ 6 ❑ 7

Rules
Guidelines, requirements, regulations, standards, "playing by the rules" . . .
    ❑ 1 ❑ 2 ❑ 3 ❑ 4 ❑ 5 ❑ 6 ❑ 7

Spontaneity
Impulsive, instinctive, improvisation, unplanned, "spur of the moment," "off the cuff," "play it by ear" . . .
    ❑ 1 ❑ 2 ❑ 3 ❑ 4 ❑ 5 ❑ 6 ❑ 7

Travel
Variety in location, on the go, on the move, "on the road again" . . .
    ❑ 1 ❑ 2 ❑ 3 ❑ 4 ❑ 5 ❑ 6 ❑ 7

Other:

❑ 1   ❑ 2   ❑ 3   ❑ 4   ❑ 5   ❑ 6   ❑ 7

Summary—Environments, Preferred Conditions:
The four to six most recurrent conditions in which I
prefer to function are . . .

(Conditions)   (Descriptors)

_____   _____

                            _____

_____   _____

                            _____

_____   _____

                            _____

_____   _____

                            _____

_____   _____

                            _____

Ends (toward which you prefer to function)—Preferred Results

Put a "✔" in each appropriate box to reveal the pattern of results you worked toward most often in your seven enjoyable accomplishments.

Making Things

A tangible product of some kind, or a personal performance—like flying an airplane, running in a race, or performing a song . . .

❑ 1　❑ 2　❑ 3　❑ 4　❑ 5　❑ 6　❑ 7

Meeting Needs

Providing the necessary information, resources, and/or know-how to address concerns, solve problems, and render service . . .

❑ 1　❑ 2　❑ 3　❑ 4　❑ 5　❑ 6　❑ 7

Moving People

Making a contribution that is aimed primarily at impacting and influencing the thoughts and behavior of others . . .

❑ 1　❑ 2　❑ 3　❑ 4　❑ 5　❑ 6　❑ 7

Summary—Ends, Preferred Results:
The result toward which I most often seem to move is . . .

_____

The second most often recurring result I am motivated toward seems to be . . .

_____

Ends—Preferred Intrinsic Rewards
Put a "✔" in the boxes that reveal the intrinsic rewards you sought in your enjoyable accomplishments.

Intrinsic Rewards
Being creative . . .
 ❑ 1 ❑ 2 ❑ 3 ❑ 4 ❑ 5 ❑ 6 ❑ 7

Being unique, different . . .
 ❑ 1 ❑ 2 ❑ 3 ❑ 4 ❑ 5 ❑ 6 ❑ 7

Gaining mastery, expertise . . .
 ❑ 1 ❑ 2 ❑ 3 ❑ 4 ❑ 5 ❑ 6 ❑ 7

Achieving quality, excellence . . .
 ❑ 1 ❑ 2 ❑ 3 ❑ 4 ❑ 5 ❑ 6 ❑ 7

Winning, beating the competition . . .
 ❑ 1 ❑ 2 ❑ 3 ❑ 4 ❑ 5 ❑ 6 ❑ 7

Overcoming obstacles, challenges . . .
 ❑ 1 ❑ 2 ❑ 3 ❑ 4 ❑ 5 ❑ 6 ❑ 7

Reaching goals, accomplishing objectives . . .
 ❑ 1 ❑ 2 ❑ 3 ❑ 4 ❑ 5 ❑ 6 ❑ 7

Learning new things . . .
 ❑ 1 ❑ 2 ❑ 3 ❑ 4 ❑ 5 ❑ 6 ❑ 7

Keeping things organized and under control . . .
 ❑ 1 ❑ 2 ❑ 3 ❑ 4 ❑ 5 ❑ 6 ❑ 7

Fulfilling requirements . . .
 ❑ 1 ❑ 2 ❑ 3 ❑ 4 ❑ 5 ❑ 6 ❑ 7

Making discoveries, uncovering new information . . .
 ❑ 1 ❑ 2 ❑ 3 ❑ 4 ❑ 5 ❑ 6 ❑ 7

Making progress . . .

❏ 1   ❏ 2   ❏ 3   ❏ 4   ❏ 5   ❏ 6   ❏ 7

Maximizing potential . . .

❏ 1   ❏ 2   ❏ 3   ❏ 4   ❏ 5   ❏ 6   ❏ 7

Acquiring, gaining ownership . . .

❏ 1   ❏ 2   ❏ 3   ❏ 4   ❏ 5   ❏ 6   ❏ 7

Making an impact . . .

❏ 1   ❏ 2   ❏ 3   ❏ 4   ❏ 5   ❏ 6   ❏ 7

Solving problems . . .

❏ 1   ❏ 2   ❏ 3   ❏ 4   ❏ 5   ❏ 6   ❏ 7

Excelling, being the best . . .

❏ 1   ❏ 2   ❏ 3   ❏ 4   ❏ 5   ❏ 6   ❏ 7

Communicating, being self-expressive . . .

❏ 1   ❏ 2   ❏ 3   ❏ 4   ❏ 5   ❏ 6   ❏ 7

Other:

❏ 1   ❏ 2   ❏ 3   ❏ 4   ❏ 5   ❏ 6   ❏ 7

Ends—Preferred Extrinsic Rewards

Put a "✔" in the boxes that reveal the extrinsic rewards you sought in your enjoyable accomplishments.

Extrinsic Rewards

Money . . .

❏ 1   ❏ 2   ❏ 3   ❏ 4   ❏ 5   ❏ 6   ❏ 7

Recognition . . .

❏ 1   ❏ 2   ❏ 3   ❏ 4   ❏ 5   ❏ 6   ❏ 7

Respect . . .
       ❑ 1   ❑ 2   ❑ 3   ❑ 4   ❑ 5   ❑ 6   ❑ 7

Reputation . . .
       ❑ 1   ❑ 2   ❑ 3   ❑ 4   ❑ 5   ❑ 6   ❑ 7

Opportunity . . .
       ❑ 1   ❑ 2   ❑ 3   ❑ 4   ❑ 5   ❑ 6   ❑ 7

Inclusion . . .
       ❑ 1   ❑ 2   ❑ 3   ❑ 4   ❑ 5   ❑ 6   ❑ 7

Response . . .
       ❑ 1   ❑ 2   ❑ 3   ❑ 4   ❑ 5   ❑ 6   ❑ 7

Responsibility . . .
       ❑ 1   ❑ 2   ❑ 3   ❑ 4   ❑ 5   ❑ 6   ❑ 7

Authority . . .
       ❑ 1   ❑ 2   ❑ 3   ❑ 4   ❑ 5   ❑ 6   ❑ 7

Freedom . . .
       ❑ 1   ❑ 2   ❑ 3   ❑ 4   ❑ 5   ❑ 6   ❑ 7

Justice . . .
       ❑ 1   ❑ 2   ❑ 3   ❑ 4   ❑ 5   ❑ 6   ❑ 7

Other:

       ❑ 1   ❑ 2   ❑ 3   ❑ 4   ❑ 5   ❑ 6   ❑ 7

Summary—Ends, Preferred Rewards:
The two to three most recurrent *intrinsic* rewards I seek
are . . .

_____

_____

_____

The two to three most recurrent *extrinsic* rewards I seek
are . . .

_____

_____

_____

THE BOTTOM LINE OF YOUR DESIGN

The purpose of fitting yourself into all those boxes you just
checked has not been to limit your identity, but to help define
it. Without a good accounting of your assets, it's impossible
for you to invest them wisely. Time now to add them all up!

Using the responses you wrote in your summary boxes,
fill in the following overview.

Functional Design Summary—Preferred Styles
Style of Processing Information
Perception   Judgment

_____   _____

_____   _____

_____   _____

Style of Problem Solving

_____   _____

Style of Producing Structure

_____   _____

_____   _____

Style of People Influencing
Function   Form

_____   _____

_____   _____

_____   _____

Functional Design Summary—Preferred Investments
Elements

_____   _____

_____   _____

_____   _____

Environments
Preferred Supervision

_____   _____

Preferred Teamwork

_____

Preferred Conditions

_____   _____

_____   _____

_____   _____

Ends
Preferred Results

_____   _____

Preferred Rewards
Intrinsic   *Extrinsic*

_____   _____

_____   _____

_____   _____

You now have a picture of your unique Functional Design—a distilled summary of the "real you," based on the real-life experiences you've had. Congratulations—you've done a lot of work! Now comes the fun part. You'll be building on what you've learned about yourself in the past few chapters—and creating a picture of opportunity for your future. In the next chapter, I'm going to ask you to dream some dreams. Close your eyes, click your heels, and start thinking about where you *really* want to be. . . .

CHAPTER EIGHT

FIELDING YOUR DREAMS
Giving Direction to Your Design

> The most pathetic person in the world
> is someone who has sight but has no vision.
>
> **Helen Keller**[1]

Whenever I begin to talk with people about their career options, there are a couple of questions I find myself asking nearly every time.

I lean back in my chair and begin with a straightforward, simple query: "You've told me that you're not satisfied with your work," I say. "So what would you like to be doing?"

You don't even have to go to graduate school to come up with that question—and almost always the same response comes back: "I'm just not sure."

But I know better than to let the matter drop there. I press forward—only this time I put a slight twist in my wording. "Well, then, tell me what you would like to do if you could put the whole picture together for yourself."

For some reason, that last phrase pushes a magic button. "Well, to be really honest," my client will say, "I *would* like to. . . ." Then a wonderful array of colorful details and data flow forth, which help me to assist the person in piecing together his dreams and honest desires into a clear picture.

Now in this brief exchange you've probably noticed, as I have, that I've actually asked the same question twice—with only one small, but critical, variation: I injected a phrase that gave my friend a sense of freedom and choice over the question of what he'd really like to do.

When it comes to our vocational direction, most of us have far more dreams and hopes and desires than we allow ourselves to express. I've found that *everyone* has a dream. Not everyone can articulate that dream. And most of us need some support to gather the courage to reach for the dreams we have. But we each have a dream.

Here's what I want to help you do in this chapter: *articulate your vocational dreams with the kind of "go for it" conviction that will help you take action to realize them.*

BELIEVE THAT YOU HAVE SOMETHING
WORTH DREAMING ABOUT

There are three basic building blocks, or "callings," on which any effective "dream planning" must be based. We've already explored the first two: a "Kingdom Calling," in which you are deeply committed to being God's representative steward of His value and truths in His world; and a "Personal Calling," in which you seek to steward your unique reflection of God's image in your own Functional Design.

The third building block in planning dreams is a "Vocational Calling." This is the identification and pursuit of your vocational vision: the clarification of your vocational dreams and desires. As you have pieced together your Functional Design in the preceding chapters, you've probably realized that your actual design is transferable to several specific types of work. Your dreams and desires are what will give focus and direction to your Functional Design.

"Delight yourself in the LORD," King David wrote, "and he

will give you the desires of your heart" (Psalm 37:4). If this is really true, as I believe it is, then as we find our pleasure in God, He plants His desires in our minds and cultivates them in our hearts.

As we walk through life in close association and obedience to God, moving at the same time toward the accomplishment of our vocational dreams and desires, we are actually participating with Him in doing what He wants done in His world. It really is appropriate to ask yourself the simple question, *"What do I want to do?"* When you line up your Functional Design with the actual dreams in the back of your mind, you'll find that much of your vocational direction is built-in. "Even as the anthropologist can examine ancient inscriptions, and divine from them the daily life of long lost people," writes Richard Bolles, "so we by examining our talents [Functional Design] and heart [Dreams and Desires] can more often than we dream, divine the Will of the Living God. For true it is, our Mission is not something He will reveal; it is something He has already revealed. It is not to be found written in the sky; it is to be found written in our members."[2]

"Getting in touch with your righteous desires provides you with knowledge of some of the most powerful forces in your life," wrote Dick Wulf in *Find Yourself, Give Yourself;* "your desires constantly guide your selection of significant tasks for the Lord."[3]

Those righteous desires take on their own particular shape in each individual. For instance, when the apostle Paul expressed his own desires for contribution he wrote, "It has always been my ambition to preach the gospel where Christ was not known, so that I would not be building on someone else's foundation" (Romans 15:20). And Paul spent his life doing precisely that, as an itinerant, tent-making evangelist.

God has a vocational contribution planned for each of us—we simply have different platforms. My ambition has been to write and consult on issues that both help and motivate Christians to take stewardship authority over their vocational contribution to this world. My friend Scott, who has been manning a desk in a Christian organization, wants to be a godly hog farmer. One person's desire for serving God is not better or less than another person's dream—just different.

Wesley's dictum "love God and do as you please" involves two sides of the same coin. As we love God, we need to be asking, "What desires has He planted in me?"

This perspective can strengthen the vitality of our faith. I have found, over and over again, that when I help individuals clarify their own dreams and desires, life takes on a new flavor, a new potency, a new potential for them. "Since I've spent some time exploring my dreams for what I want to accomplish in my world," confided my friend John, age thirty-seven, "my relationship with God has deepened dramatically. I feel like I'm alive again—real and on the raw edge of faith."

Indeed, moving forward does require faith. It means stepping out in a direction where you don't have all the answers and perhaps only a sketchy mental picture of what you'd like to do. But like Nehemiah, who wanted to rebuild the wall around Jerusalem, you need to bring that picture as clearly into focus as you can, and then explore the possibilities. You need to be able to answer the question that the Persian king demanded of Nehemiah: "What is it you want?" (Nehemiah 2:4).

DREAM YOUR OWN DREAMS

"If you do not decide what you should be doing first, other people or circumstances will decide for you," warns Rodney Laughlin.[4]

If you don't dream your own dreams, others will project their dreams onto you. Then your direction will be by default, not by choice. The only real direction you'll be headed in is around in circles.

Each of us needs to experience the freedom to voice our

hopes and dreams for our own vocational future—and to know that these personal desires can make a difference. When we have that freedom, we can take aim. Until we reach that point, there is nothing to aim at. Or, worse yet, we'll discover that what we have been aiming at is not our own target, but someone else's.

You've probably heard the saying, "If you aim at nothing you'll hit it every time." There's a lesser-known, but just as important, corollary to it: "If you aim at someone else's target, you'll lose sight of your own."

As an example, consider the case of Jane, a young woman who is well on her way to an advanced degree in interior design. She's where she wants to be now—but she sure took the long way to get there! Let's explore what happened.

All her life, Jane had loved color and design and fabric. But her father, a highly successful lawyer, had his own specific ideas about what his daughter should become. "Sometimes I think that the day I was born," Jane now comments, "my father looked into my eyes and told me I was going to go to college and get a business degree and work for a few years before I even thought about the next step. It was as if I never really had much choice in things as I was growing up. My dad loved me, but he wanted to make all my decisions for me so that I would be successful—at least in his eyes."

Redirecting her vocational contribution has not been easy for Jane. She had been aiming at someone else's target for so long that she questioned the legitimacy of her own. Yet discovering her own Functional Design and feeling the freedom to dream her own dreams has begun to open some new doors for Jane. She has entered graduate school in interior design with some confidence that she is heading in a direction that really fits her.

The Christian who lacks a sense of personal vision for her work, who has yet to clarify the mental picture of what she'd like to do in her world, lacks passion and purpose. Her work life will feel more like purgatory than a privileged cooperation with the One who made her.

Too many of us enter the work world like a baseball player climbing out of a dugout and staggering onto the playing field—so blinded by the bright light that he can't tell the pitcher's mound from home base. Without any clarity of vision, we stumble into what's immediately before us and settle for "just a job."

"I feel like I'm just floating through life," admits John, who has not yet brought his dreams and desires into focus. "At first just graduating from college and getting out into the working world was enough. It was like a breath of fresh air, like I was finally getting on with my life. But now I've been out here in the 'real world' for a while and I'm not sure where I'm headed or what I want to accomplish. I've got a job that pays the bills and supports my family, but I feel like I'm just spinning my wheels. To me it's just a job."

There is a real difference between someone who falls into just-a-job by default, and someone who chooses that situation temporarily because he knows it's a step to where he's really heading. My friend Gary is back in school to get his Ph.D. in counseling. His wife, Kim, is a flight attendant, currently on maternity leave. Gary works at three different places just to make ends meet—obviously survival jobs! He doesn't concern himself with whether or not delivering pizzas fulfills his career ambitions. Those jobs are the means to an end—not the end themselves. They are helping him fulfill his dreams of a future vocational platform from which to make his desired contribution to God's world. They are steppingstones to his future, not stopping-off points.

The difference between John and Gary is that John lacks the passion of any vocational vision for himself. He has not been free to dream. This kind of work experience is like jumping into a car to go on a long trip—without first knowing where you want to go. In such a state, it makes no difference what kind of job you have, because you lack purpose and direction.

We all have dreams inside us. But if we pay no attention to them, we'll snuff them out. We need the freedom to bring them out into the open and then act on them. "People who soar like eagles, people who live above the drag of the mediocre, are people of dreams," declares Charles Swindoll. "They have God-given drive because they have received God-given dreams."[5]

My question to you is, *What are your dreams?* In this chapter, I'd like to help you discover them.

HANDLE YOUR DREAMS WITH CARE

Before I can take you forward, I must take you back. Do you remember at about age eight or ten being asked, "What do *you* want to be when you grow up?" Most of us were asked that question many times.

If you were like my children are, most of the time you had a ready answer. You thought and dreamed about what you wanted to be. You were in a learning mode, discovering all the possibilities in life that might be yours. You were tuned into the world around you, wondering what it would be like for you to do the things you saw people around you doing. That, after all, is an accepted job description for a child—to explore her world and come up with a dream.

I watch this magical process taking place now in my own children. For the last year or so, my son Ben, now eight years old, has focused his aim on a tri-vocational career that includes "showing people around houses they're gonna buy," becoming a baseball player, and designing video games. "I got a neat idea for one while I was playing a game of Pac-Man," he says.

For some time now, our eleven-year-old Jessica has made it her ambition to become a schoolteacher or a daycare worker. Recently she's said that she wants to be a candy striper in a local hospital when she gets old enough.

I have found that giving my kids experiences that enable them to explore their world and regular opportunities to voice their dreams plays a significant part in their development as individuals. The freedom to dream and the affirmation of the process acts as a catalyst. It's like putting fertilizer on a seed that begins to sprout and take shape.

I am convinced that all of us, at one point or another in our lives, were like my children. We had all sorts of creative options popping in and out of our minds—plans and hopes and dreams bouncing around like stray Ping-Pong balls. But somewhere down the path we lost a lot of our explorer's heart. Someone mentioned that we couldn't make much money as a daycare worker. Or our sixth-grade soccer team lost the city championship and we gave up the idea of becoming a sports broadcaster. Whatever, wherever, whoever—something put a damper on our dreams until we just quit dreaming.

But if that's the case for you, take heart! All is not lost. I'm going to give you a well-deserved opportunity to dream again—and to put those dreams into words.

Two exercises follow. The first is like a jump start to get you thinking about and exploring common ground in the different jobs "out there" that appeal to you.

The second exercise is designed to stimulate you to envision the details of your current vocational dream. I say "current" because dreams change. Your vocational calling is not set in cement. The desires for contribution that God has put on your heart may very well change over the course of time.

Before you start, I recommend that you make several photocopies for your personal use of the pages on which these exercises appear. You may profit most from making these exercises an extended assignment, keeping your drafts tucked into this book for future use. You'll benefit from reworking your efforts as you gain clarity regarding your vocational direction, or experience shifts in your vocational desires.

Exercise One: Exploring
Note: There are at least four ways to discover information about various jobs: (1) reading (your local library has many

reference books describing thousands of different jobs—try starting with the *Dictionary of Occupational Titles,* published by the U.S. Dept. of Labor); (2) observing different jobs firsthand; (3) interviewing people about their work (ask questions about what they do, what they enjoy and dislike, how they got involved, etc.); and (4) experiencing—trying by actually doing different types of work (e.g., volunteering your time in various functions, taking on a part-time job to explore a particular field).

Q: What jobs have you seen or heard about that appeal to you? Why?

Example: Weather forecaster on television, because he gathers information . . . is called upon to share it with others . . . has a specialized focus . . . is considered an expert in his field.

■

■

■

■

■

■

■

■

Summary: What similarities, or common themes, do you discover among these jobs?

■

■

■

■

■

Exercise Two: Envisioning

Q: If time and money were not an issue, what would you like to be doing vocationally over the next five to seven years?

Note: You needn't give this job a title. What functions would you be performing? What issues, needs, challenges, or opportunities would you be addressing? What sort of context would you be operating in?

ONE FOR THE ROAD

As you finish up this process of articulating your dreams, there is one woman in particular I'd like you to keep in mind. She provides an example of the better outcomes that can result from gathering the courage to dream about your best vocational niche.

Kathy was a highly trained registered nurse who, although she had worked in her field for several years, had been experiencing less and less fulfillment in her chosen career direction. She wasn't desperate—just discouraged enough to seek help.

In the process of discovering her Functional Design, Kathy also was required to put her vocational dreams and desires down on paper. "But what I'd really like to do," she insisted at the time, "is something I've never seen being done anywhere. It's just this picture I have in my mind. So what's the use?"

"That's not the point," I countered. "Put aside what's out there and write down what's in here," I said, pointing to her head. "What's your dream? Your desires? What would you like to do in your world if you could design it yourself?"

"But I'm not the entrepreneurial type," she protested. "I need to fit into something already going on somewhere."

"What 'something'? Doing what and where?" I pressed her further.

She began to get the point. I wasn't asking her to become something she wasn't. I was asking her to tell me what she wanted to do, the details of what she wanted to accomplish, and the contribution she desired to make.

So Kathy finally put it down on paper. In the process, of course, her mind continued to present her with all the reasons why this was going to be a waste of time—but she ignored them. She wrote out the details and specifics of what she really wanted to do—of a job that would draw on all her God-given resources and would lead to the outcomes she hoped to achieve.

In a sense, Kathy simply prepared herself for opportunity. When it knocked, she was ready. Today she's wonderfully motivated in her new position within a local hospital as a Patient Representative, functioning as a resource and liaison between the hospital administration and individuals with health care problems.

Listen to what Kathy wrote me: "All that assessing and exploring stuff from two years ago has finally paid off," she said. "I've just landed a job that's really what I wanted all along and wouldn't have known it—unless I had taken the time to think and dream. For the first time in years, I can't wait to get to work each morning and have at it!"

I hope that in a few years you can write a letter like Kathy's. I hope you'll know yourself and your dreams so well that when opportunity comes knocking, on whatever door and to whatever degree that door begins to open, you'll be prepared to walk right on through.

When I Grow Up

When I grow up
I could be a doc
I could help people
with the chicken pock.
Or else a teach
but instead of an apple
I'd want a peach
Or even a judge
but I'd like to judge fudge
But I can't
make up my mind,
so I will be kind
and I will find
a perfect career for me.

—Jessica Anne Frähm, age eleven

CHAPTER NINE

R.S.V.P.

Responding to Your Dreams by Setting Goals and Taking Action

Many people have the right aims in life.
They just never get around to pulling the trigger.[1]

Shortly after I began work on the writing of this book, my wife, Anne, was hospitalized upon discovery of an advanced state of breast cancer that had been misdiagnosed for nearly a year.

The pain in her back assumed to be the nagging reminder of an earlier car accident was something far more ominous. Anne had cancer—cancer that had spread from her breast to her bones.

Her doctor tried his best to be kind. On the day he sat down to inform us, he spoke reassuringly of the latest medical advances, of the importance of keeping a positive mental attitude. But I could tell he was leading up to something.

He leaned back in his chair for a moment, as though he was trying to distance himself from something painful. Then he said, "I'm afraid, though, Mrs. Frähm, I have to admit to

155

you that most people who have what you have die within two years."

I felt my hands turn cold and clammy. The color drained out of my wife's face like a pink shirt suddenly bleached white. For what seemed like an eternal moment, we sat speechless, trying to absorb the impact of his words.

As soon as the doctor left, a thousand questions and emotions engulfed us like a thick fog, swallowing up our lives and leaving us groping our way into an unknown future. How could this be? Why was this happening? What would we do? How long *did* we have? How would life change?

As Anne recuperated in the hospital from surgery, I spent several lonely, hollow nights at home, feeling my guts tied in knots and my heart being wrenched right out of my chest. I was shattered and numb on the inside, yet trying to be strong on the outside for our children.

One morning, after a particularly hard night at home, I arrived at my wife's hospital bed to find her freshly showered, her makeup on, and her personal journal open on her lap.

"Honey," she said, "last night I lay awake for a long time wrestling with a lot of questions. I wanted assurance that at least one person has had what I have and has survived long term."

Wiping away a tear and pulling her Bible to her lap, she continued, "but I'm not sure I can count on getting any such assurance. I'm faced with actually living out what I've always known in my head—that there are no guarantees for any of us, that each of us should live life as if today were our last."

She stopped there, as if to allow the force of that statement—so well known and so little lived—to penetrate the moment.

"It wouldn't be good for us to keep life on hold for the next couple of years to see if I can beat this. That would be two years wasted. Let's make the most of what we've got. I've written out in my journal my dreams and desires for how I'd like to make the best use of whatever time God has left on His agenda for me. I've written out what I want to accomplish, and I've set down some goals to shoot for. Will you help me?"

What Anne said that morning made so much sense that I knew God had led her to those words.

I did help her, and together we came up with three steps that would give her a true sense of moving forward in her life, of reaching goals. We planned some ways that she could make some strokes in our children's lives. We listed the projects she still longed to see completed around our house. And we discussed how best to begin her third dream: to set up the basics of her own business. Like the little girl who made forts out of weeds in her back yard, Anne had always wanted to help people design the interiors of their homes.

Over the months, as the possibility of death has overshadowed us, I have learned some very important lessons from my wife about living. For one thing, I have ceased to think of her as being in a whole separate category, quarantined among those unfortunate enough to have a potentially terminal illness. More and more I realize that Anne is living out the reality of my life, too—and everyone else I know—only more visibly. We all have expiration dates stamped on our containers. Life itself is risky, and I've never met anyone who has survived it.

We all have a beginning and an ending—or maybe this is a better way to say it: We all have a beginning, and God offers us an even greater beginning. But in between we need to make the most of the time we've been given. Like an Oreo cookie, the stuff in the middle matters immensely!

That's why the apostle Paul told people who were grappling with how God wanted them to invest themselves to live "not as unwise but as wise, making the most of every opportunity, because the days are evil" (Ephesians 5:15-16).

For the Christian who is looking to God to give her direction, "making the most of every opportunity" encompasses every aspect of her life, including her work. You and I must keep moving forward in the light God has given us: our dreams and desires for contribution.

AN INCH AT A TIME

Too often we live as if clarifying what we *really* want to do with our lives must always remain a future project. We tell ourselves that once we have more time or more money or the kids are grown up or the interest rates have come down—whenever things are just right—then we will make some changes.

But a lifetime is really not much more than one day repeated over and over again many times. To effect real change in our vocational direction, there comes a day when we must begin to take steps—even the smallest steps—down another road. Just like my wife did, we need to set some goals and then start taking the steps.

It's easier, though, to complain in the security of the known, than to willingly chart a course of action into the unknown. And let's face it—taking control of your vocational direction can be risky. One thing is sure—if we're going to move forward in some new directions, we will have to grow comfortable with the element of risk.

An Old Testament story from Numbers 13 features the kind of faith required to move out in new directions. Here the Bible records the history of how God led the wandering nation of Israel into His assigned place for them in His world: the land of Canaan. The plan was set up in such a way that the Israelites were to move in and take ownership despite whatever hurdles seemed to present themselves. The Lord would take care of the rest.

So, the away team was sent forth on a reconnaissance mission to check the place out. Upon their return and debriefing, each acknowledged the merits of the property in mind. But almost to a man, their reports were filled with gloomy forecasts based on the tremendous size of the obstacles blocking the planned takeover.

Of the twelve-man research team, only two offered reports that gave any credence to the viablity of such an undertaking. They, too, saw and acknowledged the roadblocks. But what they did that the others didn't—what they would that others wouldn't—was to go back to the original leading that the "Boss" had given them.

"There are giants in that land," was the complaint that echoed most often from tent to tent those days in the wandering nation of Israel, as they cowered outside the borders of what God intended for them.

In a strikingly similar way, we often tend to hold back from entering new and unfamiliar territory in our vocational lives—even when we deeply long to make a change.

As a career consultant I've identified at least three giants that keep Christians sitting on the borders of their own vocational dreams and desires, reluctant and fearful to take the steps that would move them forward into contributions God has put on their hearts: what others think, how long it takes, and how much it costs.

THE OPINIONS OF OTHERS

I've already tried to slay the first giant for you. Let's take another look, just to make sure he's really dead. I call him "the opinions of others."

The opinions of others surround us daily. They have the potential to be both a blessing and a curse, a help or a hindrance. Sometimes the insights that others offer us can be just what we need to hear in order to make wise career decisions. At other times such well-meaning "counsel" can throw us so far off course that it takes years to regain our bearings.

Not long ago I interviewed a man in his forties who was in the middle of a sabbatical from teaching college. "I'm just not sure I'm going in the right direction in life," he said over a cup of coffee. "To tell you the truth, I've never really enjoyed teaching that much. I'm seriously considering going back to school and starting out in a new direction."

As we sat there in the coffee shop, I had him tell me about the things he'd done in life that he really enjoyed and that had given him some sense of personal accomplishment. (Does this sound familiar?) His voice became excited and his actions animated as he served up one story after another to someone like me who was as eager to feast on the facts of his history as he was to dish them out.

The ingredients of his accomplishments began to repeat themselves—things like reading and researching, presenting facts through presentations and verbal arguments, coming up against competition and beating it. These elements showed up again and again.

After six or eight entrees of his enjoyable accomplishments, I made an observation. "To me," I interjected, "it sounds like you would have made quite a good lawyer, among other things."

"That's interesting," he replied. "I was in law school for three years and thoroughly enjoyed it. But eventually I switched my major to teaching."

"Is that right?" I asked, more than a little interested in what had made him switch from something that seemed so right for him. "What made you change you mind?"

He said, "I became a Christian at the end of my third year." I nearly croaked.

"The guy that led me to Christ," he continued, "had strong feelings that a person could not hold Christian values and be a lawyer at the same time. I admired his wisdom in other areas, so I switched. He was a teacher and convinced me that teaching was where a person could really have an impact. Now I'm thinking about going back to school to get that law degree I once pursued. I look forward to the challenge of representing Christ in a realm of our culture that perhaps we Christians have shied away from too long."

Do you understand why I'm sharing this man's story with you? Unless you decide for yourself what you'd like to contribute to this world, others have a way of wanting to decide that for you.

There is in each of us the tendency to impose upon others

our own design and desires. We point them down the paths most familiar to us, the ways along which we found our own fit, our own "niche." *But instead of helping the individual make sense of his own God-given road map, we often make him follow ours.*

The result, of course, is a confused individual who is living out someone else's life and vision rather than his own.

Wherever there is a "teacher-student" or "leader-follower" or "counselor-counselee" sense of relationship, there is always the potential that the input of the first party will overshadow the God-designed individuality and personal decision-making of the second. In the realm of vocational selection, this can lead to a tragic waste of human potential.

Good career counseling always seeks to recognize and avoid the counselor's bias toward certain directions in order to focus clearly on the one being counseled. It always starts with the individual, a thorough understanding of how God has designed him and what desires for contribution God has planted within him.

Once these twin foundations of vocational stewardship (design and desire) are firmly in place, then the thoughts, opinions, and input of others can be immensely helpful. Brainstorming ideas with others and networking with them concerning opportunities they're aware of that fit the individual may open up new awareness of vocational doors to knock on.

In fact, once you're able to explain to others the kind of work you're interested in, you ought to ask them to "lend you their ears." Get them listening for opportunities within their own spheres of work that might fit your design and fulfill your desires. It has been shown that nearly eighty percent of all job openings in this country go unpublicized. People hear about them by word of mouth. The larger your network of informed individuals interested in helping you, the better.

But again let me emphasize that the stewardship and decisions concerning your vocational direction in life are *yours.* Alan Bloom, author of *The Closing of the American Mind,* made a statement in a *Time* magazine article that applies well in this context: "A thoughtless man," he said, "will be controlled by the thoughts of another."[2]

You and I must think and plan for our contribution to this world. We must take upon ourselves personal ownership of and vision for our work. That's what it means to be God's co-worker in His world. That's what R.S.V.P.—"representative stewardship vocational planning"—is all about.

TIME

The second giant that blocks our freedom to live according to our own unique design is *time.* In particular, I'm referring to the common excuse that "I'm too old . . . I've been doing this far too long to change now."

I'd like to know, How old is "too old" to make changes, to head in new directions, to develop a new vision for how we might contribute to this world through our work?

"I'm already fifty," a client recently said. "Wouldn't it be just as well for me to grit my teeth and grunt it out in this job for another fifteen years since I'm close to retirement anyway?"

I do indeed groan when I hear people talk that way about the years of the only life they'll ever be given to live. "Grunt it out for another fifteen," he said. I wanted to ask him which he was doing: working at a job or doing time in jail until his parole came up?

Sure, it's not easy to change directions or to start all over again when you're fifty. But "easy" isn't the issue. It's a matter of, Would it be right to take the risks to move toward a better investment of your "self" in God's world of work?

It's always refreshing to meet someone like Dorothy, who at age seventy-seven refuses to let life pass her by. Like Thoreau would say, Dorothy is still "sucking the marrow out of life."

In the last year I've received three personal letters from

her. In the first she told of how she had just sold the gift shop she and her husband had owned and run until his recent death:

> I closed out the shop and have carved out a new niche
> for myself. I had several interviews and finally ended
> up with the greatest opportunity of all. I work as a
> volunteer with Volunteer Services as a contact per-
> son. Basically, I prepare newspaper publicity and
> speak at mobile home parks in an effort to motivate
> residents to stop being couch potatoes and meet
> the world once more. Most of them have had great
> experiences working but have laid their talents and
> interests aside.

In her second letter, Dorothy told me about the college courses she was taking:

> I'll be at the University of Wisconsin in Stevens Point.
> I meet so many exciting people, all eager to learn and
> not ready to admit that they are "old" except in body.
> We live in the dormitory and have regular university
> professors.

In Dorothy's third letter, she explained her new vocational adventure:

> I resigned at the peak of my work with Volunteer
> Services. I'm now starting an independent service for
> my church. I'm no spring chicken, but I know work
> that needs to be done for others when I see it. I have
> spoken to the congregation, have completed a talent
> file for work within the church, and am now working
> on a skills bank for community work within the areas
> of health, welfare, and education. Just today I mailed
> out letters to fifty-five nonprofit organizations in the

community telling them about our work. To me, the necessity of speaking to the concerns of others is my calling.

When are we too old to hunt for our niche in God's world of work? When we're six feet underground! Dorothy realizes that if she just sits back and lets the grass grow under her feet, before long it will be growing *over* her feet.

Don't let the time giant stomp all over your attempts to live in harmony with the way God made you.

MONEY

Money—perhaps the largest and most troublesome giant of all. For many of us, this one is especially tough to kill off.

"Money can't buy you happiness," it's been said, "but it goes a long way toward easing the pain." It's hard to get around the reality that we all need money to survive, especially in a consumer culture such as ours.

The Bible exhorts us to provide for our families and for the responsibilities God has entrusted to us. But what does that mean? What level of lifestyle does that require or allow? I'm not sure I have an answer to that question. In the final analysis, each family must decide for itself.

Dave and Sue, friends of ours, had to deal with the question of money and lifestyle as they faced Dave's growing frustration within his career direction of marketing research. With two kids and a mortgage, it wasn't easy to send Dave back to graduate school.

Dave and Sue are working together as a team to balance the demands of parenting, homemaking, Dave's schooling, and Sue's part-time job. "We've sold our home, uprooted our family, and taken a fifty percent cut in our income," says Sue, "but it's worth it to see Dave pursuing something he really enjoys. The fact is, we're enjoying the change and the challenge of living with less."

I appreciate the example this couple has set. They made

the conscious decision that they valued their work on some other basis than the money it paid. Proverbs 16:9 reads, "In his heart a man plans his course, but the LORD determines his steps." All too often I find that the principle at work in people's lives is, "In his heart a man plans his course, but money determines his steps."

"My dad hated his job the whole time I was growing up," said a woman in a Niche Hunt seminar. "To his credit he kept at it because he wanted to give the family a certain lifestyle. But you know, I would have gladly traded it all if I could've had a happier dad."

Does that hit you the way it hits me? Money and certain standards of living just can't purchase what we really want and need from life.

I'm not advocating that you automatically go for jobs that pay you less. I am pointing out that many of us let the issues surrounding money and lifestyle get in the way of the contributions we want to make to this world. We seem to be better at finding ways to squelch the dreams God has given us than accomplishing them. It takes courage to step out in the direction of our dreams.

For many years Cy and Debbie were on the pastoral staff of a large church. As he approached forty, Cy began to dream of entering the mainstream of the business world. He and Debbie saw it as a more effective channel for influencing people in the ways they believed God was leading them.

Together Cy and Debbie agreed to start out on a new venture. The complexity of the undertaking was overwhelming. It involved moving to a new city, reorienting their four children, and trading in the security and significance of a church staff position for a part-time job at UPS—not to mention balancing the multiple demands in Cy's full-time enrollment in the Ph.D. program of an esteemed university.

Not many of us have the same capacity as Cy and Debbie, but we do have the same God. Money was a concern for them, as it is for all of us. But they did not let the lack of it deter them from finding ways and means to move toward their dreams.

TAKING STEPS

In chapter 5, I introduced you to my eight-year-old son, Benjamin David Frähm. This morning as I write, moving toward my long-term goal of bringing this book to completion, Ben is up in his room trying to move toward his long-term goal of cleaning up his room.

Ben is not yet adept in the fine art of breaking down the bigger objective into smaller, more accessible goals. All he can see when he approaches the wasteland he refers to as his bedroom are the multitude of obstacles that lie in the way of achieving his final goal of a clean room. His difficulty in identifying and acting on smaller goals within the bigger picture tends to paralyze him. He is easily distracted by whatever comes along—ultimately getting no closer to his overall goal and increasing his frustration with the whole project.

If I know my son, he'll be down here within the next fifteen minutes wanting to know if he can finish up tomorrow without even getting started today. And if I let him do that, tomorrow will never come. It happens every time. If I don't help him see those smaller increments by which he can measure his progress toward what seems to be a monumental undertaking, he will never get started.

Most people searching for a more appropriate vocation seem able to identify the big picture of what they'd like to be doing five years into the future. But it's the *getting there* that leaves them lost, frustrated, and finally ready to give up. They don't outline the incremental steps which, if systematically taken, will move them toward their goal.

Unless you plan out a series of steps that will take you in the direction of your vocational goal and in the process give you a steady sense of accomplishment, you may never reach your destination. The old adage says it best: "The journey of a thousand miles begins with one step."

Let me share with you some of the various steps that I've seen others take in their own niche hunt. Perhaps you'll find that some of them apply to your own situation.

■ *Investigate the possibility of renegotiating your job description where you are now.* Is it possible for you to change job descriptions in order to move further toward what you'd really like to do, without leaving your present company or employer?

Employers and supervisors don't like to lose good people. If you have a clear idea of the directional changes you'd like to make in your vocational investment, explore the in-house possibilities first. Probably more often than you think, a clear and thoughtful proposal built upon the facts of your own self-knowledge may reach a listening ear. Employers will often redesign jobs or create new ones in to order to enhance employees' productivity.

When considering change in your job description, ask yourself, "How might I accomplish my dream and remain with this company at the same time?" Once you answer that, put it in writing by way of a proposed job description. Ask for an appointment with whomever you report to, offering your thoughts as "a proposal for how I might best serve this company in the future."

Kathy works for a power company. Her initial job there was helping in the administration of accounts by keeping track of payments and other important data. In the process, she developed a keen interest in the actual workings of various computer programs and systems functions. Eventually, she decided that she'd like to refocus her contribution. She drew up a proposal and offered it to her supervisor. In this proposal, she outlined her desires and the skills in computer systems management that she'd acquired out of personal interest and ambition.

"That's interesting," her supervisor responded. "We were just about to call in an expert to help us with this particular problem. Why don't you take a look at it for us?" Kathy did. She solved the problem and won herself a new position in the company.

Many employers are unaware of the hidden resources within their own companies. Unless you tell your employer what you have and would like to offer, you may remain one of those hidden people.

If your current employer offers no possibility for follow-through or negotiation on your proposal, your effort has not been wasted. You have done your "on the scene" exploration and have at least moved ahead in the process of informed elimination. All too often, though, we shut the doors of opportunity on ourselves by assuming they won't open before we even try.

■ *Find someone who is doing the kind of work you'd like to do and conduct an information-seeking interview.* Talking to someone who has gone down the same path you're aiming for can increase your awareness of the steps and hurdles that lie ahead of you in your transition. Try asking an experienced person the following questions: What do you enjoy most about what you do? What do you enjoy least? In your opinion, what sort of personal qualities make a person well-suited to this kind of work? What personal qualities might be liabilities in this field? What is involved in an average work week for you? What type of educational background or training do you have for your job? What would you recommend for someone just entering the field? What sort of strategy did you use to find and secure employment in this field? Did you use a résumé? Would you be willing to let me look at the form you used in your résumé? A note about résumés: There are two major formats for résumés in common use in the work world, the "chronological" and the "functional." I prefer the latter for reasons discussed in the appendix of this book.

When my wife was working on entering the realm of interior decorating she interviewed several other women who were already involved in this line of work. Her particular question centered around credentials: Would she need a degree in interior decorating in order to attract customers? On the whole, their counsel was that she would not. Her background as an art major gave her sufficient credibility to get at least a foothold in the field.

"It gave me a great deal of reassurance to hear this from

women already working in this field," recounts Anne. "I knew that I had the necessary gifts and abilities necessary, but marketing myself was a question."

■ *Develop a personal Niche Hunt Network.* People in transition need a support group—not only for emotional support, but for the wealth of information and assistance that such a group can supply.

Once you've identified a clear picture of who you are and what it is you'd really like to be doing over the next five to seven years, then you should get other people involved with you as your agents.

One way to do this is to host a "Great Niche Hunt" party in your home. Invite a group of your friends, order pizza, and have a brainstorm session. Start by telling your friends the details of how you function best and the dreams you have for the future. You might even hand out one-page descriptions of the job you're looking for. Then ask everyone in the group for ideas, possibilities, and names of people you might contact as you keep track of them on a big flip chart.

You may be amazed at the number of leads you end up with. Not only that, but your friends have now become a motivated board of directors for your company of one. Asking them for involvement like this in your life will stimulate their personal interest in your success.

At the end of every Great Niche Hunt seminar I teach, I have the participants gather in small groups and do this sort of brainstorming and resource sharing with each other. One woman in career transition was having a hard time coming up with ideas about where she might invest her love of reading and her knowledge of books. She's now employed as a customer relations specialist by a local publisher. "I'd never have thought of that until someone in our group mentioned it as a possibility," she said.

Make use of these three good ideas about how to get started in taking steps toward your vocational future. Once you get going, you'll probably think of more. What's most important, however, is that you do start—and then keep going. If we sit around waiting for the right conditions or for assurance that our results will be successful, the wise author of Ecclesiastes tells us, we'll never get anything done (11:1-6).

In the last chapter you spent some time identifying your vocational vision—a picture of what you'd like to be doing. Now it's time to respond to that invitation to your future. Make several copies of the following chart for your personal use, keeping track of the steps you need to take and the progress you've made toward your goal.

R.S.V.P. (Representative Stewardship Vocational Planning)—Steps:

Q: What steps can you identify that would move you ahead toward your vision of what you'd like to be doing vocationally over the next five to seven years?

■ Step to take:

■ Progress made:

■ Step to take:

■ Progress made:

■ Step to take:

■ Progress made:

■ Step to take:

■ Progress made:

MOVING AHEAD WITHOUT MANDATING

Over the course of this year I have watched my wife take small but significant steps toward the dreams and goals she feels that God has laid on her heart. Anne has helped Ben find his niche in soccer and Jessica begin to play the clarinet. She has orchestrated some wonderful family memories—time together doing special things we've always wanted to do. We have knocked out walls, redesigned bathrooms, painted and wallpapered galore. She has put together her first brochure for the interior decorating service she wants to offer. She has not let any grass grow under her feet.

What challenges me, though, and the reason that I feel so instructed by Anne's life, is that she took these steps toward her goals in the midst of the deep fatigue of chemotherapy. Soon she will be traveling to Omaha, Nebraska, for a nine-week program of radically intensified chemotherapy with a bone marrow transplant. When she goes she won't be laying her dreams aside, she'll be taking them with her.

Anne is intimately aware of the uncertainty of her future. She knows that there may be a different script written for her life than the one she hopes for. But she is willing to take the steps needed today and trust God for her future, because she knows that anyone who ceases to dream has already begun to die.

The truth that Anne is living "out loud" is one of life's great paradoxes. She has learned the necessity of pursuing her dreams and yet, all the while, maintaining the inner flexibility of allowing God the freedom in her life to shape and reshape those dreams as He sees fit. David said, "The LORD will fulfill his purpose for me; your love, O LORD, endures forever — do not abandon the works of your hands" (Psalm 138:8).

Someone has likened the individual Christian to a boat. Our dreams are what unleash us from the dock and get us moving out on the open waters of life. Once we're in motion, the Lord steers us in directions that match the goals He has intended for us. As Solomon says, "We should make plans, counting on God to direct us" (Proverbs 16:9, TLB).

The real truth is that we never know what's around the next bend in the journey. I would never have envisioned the possibility that my good friend Bryan Dixon would fall off a ladder and die. Yet I know that God used that tragedy to alter the direction of my life — especially in a vocational sense.

The occurrence of my wife's cancer blindsided me as well. But what we've learned and experienced in the process of dealing with this disease — about God, about life, and about ourselves — has radically reshaped our lives. It may seem odd, but we have experienced great blessing in the midst of great pain.

What Anne and I have discovered is that life, as God meant it to be lived, is a partnership — a collaborative effort between the Lord and us. You and I have to live in harmony with Him. We need to identify the design He has given us, follow the dreams of our hearts, and take action toward our goals. But at the same time, we must always allow Him to steer the boat. He knows exactly where He wants us to go and what's up ahead.

I hope that this confidence in God's guidance is one of the most important discoveries of your own hunt for a place of belonging in your world. May your life express true "rhyme and reason" as God's poetry in motion in the niche He has created you to fill.

A Psalm of Life

Tell me not, in mournful numbers,
　　Life is but an empty dream! —
For the soul is dead that slumbers,

And things are not what they seem.
Life is real! Life is earnest!
And the grave is not its goal;
Dust thou art, to dust returnest,
Was not spoken of the soul.
Not enjoyment, and not sorrow
Is our destined end or way;
But to act, that each tomorrow
Find us farther than today.
Art is long, and Time is fleeting,
And our hearts, though stout and brave,
Still, like muffled drums, are beating
Funeral marches to the grave.
In the world's broad field of battle,
In the bivouac of life,
Be not like dumb, driven cattle!
Be a hero in the strife!
Trust no Future, howe'er pleasant!
Let the dead Past bury its dead!
Act—act in the living Present!
Heart within, and God o'erhead!
Lives of great men all remind us
We can make our lives sublime,
And, departing, leave behind us
Footprints on the sand of time—
Footprints, that perhaps another,
Sailing o'er life's solemn main,
A forlorn and shipwrecked brother,
Seeing, shall take heart again.
Let us, then, be up and doing,
With a heart for any fate;
Still achieving, still pursuing,
Learn to labor and to wait.

—Henry Wadsworth Longfellow[3]

APPENDIX
Creating a Functional Résumé

The functional résumé provides the logical strategy for integrating the details of your Functional Design and your dreams and desires into a system for marketing your desired contribution to God's world of work.

Regardless of your current vocational context, developing a well-tuned résumé of this type will allow you to see your value and unique potential. It will increase your confidence in representing yourself to present or potential employers, thus giving you a sense of greater personal stewardship and career flexibility. Even if you are planning to launch out on your own as an entrepreneur, creating this sort of résumé will help you to set your objective and prove to yourself that you have what it takes to accomplish it.

The first step in creating this sort of self-marketing tool is to decide on a *job objective*: a simple statement describing the kind of work function you'd like to perform. To do this, of course, you'll be drawing on the dreams and desire you've already identified. What is it that you want to do? *A résumé without a job objective is like a car without gas.* It may look nice, but it'll get you nowhere! As a one-time personnel director, I can tell you that if you don't know what you want to do for me, I won't have the time *or desire* to figure it out for you. If you leave off your job objective on purpose in order to be considered for anything that is open, nothing is probably what you'll get.

The second step is to show via your selected accomplishments that you possess the *strengths* to fulfill the requirements of the job objective you've chosen to make your aim. Look back through the chapters in this book that focused on your design. What patterns of your functioning would you most like to emphasize in light of the job objective? What accomplishments in your past best showcase these?

Be brief, yet detailed. An accomplishment, such as "Put together a staff manual for the employees of a conference center," has more punch if you add just a few details— "created and produced a fifty-page staff manual for the 110 employees of a 300-bed conference center."

If you find yourself inclined toward several different job objectives, develop a specially tailored functional résumé for each. Of your many accomplishments, list those that highlight the strengths you most enjoy using as specifically related to the job objective at the top of each résumé.

Following are two different styles within the functional résumé approach. In each case, the person has brought strategic details and expressions of his or her Functional Design to bear on the chosen job objective.

You'll notice that this special layout and approach allows emphasis of strengths and work accomplishments, while drawing lesser attention to educational background. This can be important if you're marketing yourself toward a job objective unrelated to your formal education, which is true of both examples.

Even if you are marketing yourself toward a job within a field related to your degree, a functional résumé will help your potential employer identify the unique strengths and qualifications you'd bring to the job.

If you'd like more information on this sort of résumé, I'm a big fan of *The Damn Good Resume Guide* by Yana Parker, published by Ten Speed Press. It's excellent!

Jean N. Conner
3600 North Summer Avenue
Colorado Springs, Colorado 80909
(719) 555-4770 (Home) or 555-2112 (Work)

OBJECTIVE: A position as Office Manager in a financial consulting firm offering opportunity for professional development.

HIGHLIGHTS OF QUALIFICATIONS
- Over ten years experience leading/supervising people.
- Extensive experience in public speaking.
- Skilled in planning and organizing.
- Five years administrative experience in office setting.

PROFESSIONAL EXPERIENCE
Directing and Managing
- Supervised thirty people in work-study program.
- Directed youth program, setting direction and overseeing staff of twenty-five.
- Developed entire spectrum of job descriptions, monitoring their implementation.
- Selected and trained five supervisors.

Master Planning
- Planned and organized over 100 national and local conference meetings.
- Envisioned, planned, and implemented conference programming and policies, which subsequently became the prototype for all such conferences.

Promoting and Consulting
- Gave promotional and educational presentations more than thirty times in five different states.
- Trained eighty people in public speaking and small group facilitation.
- Addressed audiences of over 250 on six different occasions.
- Developed a seminar on financial management, successfully presenting it in group and one-on-one settings.
- Started cottage industry business, promoting products and consulting with clients.

EMPLOYMENT HISTORY
1987-present	Administrative Assistant to U.S. Director of The Navigators
1982-1987	Director of Women's Ministries (local), The Navigators
1980-1982	Secretary to Director of Student Teaching, University of Illinois
1979-1980	Secretary, University of Illinois

EDUCATION
B.A., Christian Education, Wheaton College, 1979

David R. Hinson
14010-125th Place Southwest
Seattle, Washington 98030
(206) 555-3700

JOB OBJECTIVE: Administrative Assistant in Business or Education

STRENGTHS

Managing Information: gathering, organizing, analyzing, synthesizing, standardizing

ACCOMPLISHMENTS

■ Created and produced a fifty-page staff manual for the 110 employees of a 300-bed conference center.
■ Directed student admissions for an eighty-student training institute, creating and implementing a procedure manual for the admissions department.
■ Coordinated classroom use documentation and class registration.
■ Researched taxes on real estate for a title insurance company.

Managing Projects: organizing logistics and resources, coordinating effort of others

■ Coordinated finances, promotion, and event logistics for a fund-raising event, which raised $8000.
■ Organized four retreats for 110 employees of a conference center.
■ Coordinated finances, correspondence with speakers, room preparation, and registration for fifteen one-day seminars, involving a total of more than 1000 attenders.
■ Chaired a committee of eight computer specialists responsible for planning and decision-making on current computer needs of conference center and training institute.
■ Supervised staff person responsible for payroll and benefits administration.

Performing computer skills and functions

■ Proficient in WordPerfect and WordStar with working knowledge of Lotus 1-2-3.
■ Experienced in the use of IBM and CP/M computers.
■ Performed bookkeeping and accounts payable functions.

WORK HISTORY

1986-1988 *Personnel Administrator*
Glen Eyrie Conference Center,
Colorado Springs, Colorado

1984-1986 *Tax Researcher*
Tucker Title Insurance, Seattle, Washington

EDUCATION

Bachelor of Arts in Psychology
Western Washington University

NOTES

Chapter One: When Feeling Bad About Work Is Good

1. Ralph Mattson and Arthur Miller, *Finding a Job You Can Love* (Nashville, TN: Thomas Nelson Publishers, 1982), page 123.
2. Susan Littwin, *The Postponed Generation* (New York: William Morrow, 1987), page 30.
3. Lisa Heiser, as quoted by Lawrence Kutner, "College Seniors Confused by Career Choices," *New York Times News Service*.
4. Elizabeth Dole, acceptance speech as Secretary of Labor, Washington, DC, January 30, 1989.

Chapter Two: Priests in Work Clothes

1. John R. W. Stott, "Reclaiming the Biblical Doctrine of Work," *Christianity Today*, May 4, 1979, pages 36-37.

2. Stott, page 36.
3. Larry Peabody, *Secular Work Is Full-Time Service* (Fort Washington, PA: Christian Literature Crusade, 1974), page 73.
4. Grace Noll Crowell, "The Common Tasks," in *Poems That Touch the Heart,* compiled by A. L. Alexander (New York: Doubleday, 1941), page 256.

Chapter Three: The Stewardship of Self
1. Saint Augustine, as quoted by Dr. Paul Brand and Philip Yancey, *Fearfully and Wonderfully Made* (Grand Rapids, MI: Zondervan, 1980), introduction.
2. Douglas LaBier, *Modern Madness: The Emotional Fallout of Success* (Reading, MA: Addison-Wesley, 1986), page 33.
3. Littwin, *Postponed Generation,* page 34.
4. Rodney S. Laughlin, *The Job Hunter's Handbook* (Waco, TX: Word Books, 1985), page 132.

Chapter Four: Going Back for the Future
1. Martin E. Clark, *Choosing Your Career* (Grand Rapids, MI: Baker Book House, 1987), page 26.
2. Richard Bolles, *What Color Is Your Parachute?* (Berkeley, CA: Ten Speed Press, 1990), pages 224-225.

Chapter Six: Preferred Investments
1. Bolles, *What Color Is Your Parachute?* pages 262-263.
2. Mattson and Miller, *Finding a Job You Can Love,* pages 61, 67.
3. Frederick Herzburg, *Work and the Nature of Man* (Cleveland, OH: The World Publishing Co., 1966), page 72.

Chapter Eight: Fielding Your Dreams
1. Helen Keller, from *The Speaker's Sourcebook,* compiled by Glen Van Ekeren (Englewood Cliffs, NJ: Prentice Hall, 1988), page 182.
2. Bolles, *What Color Is Your Parachute?* page 404.
3. Dick Wulf, *Find Yourself, Give Yourself* (Colorado Springs, CO: NavPress, 1983, out of print), page 152.

4. Laughlin, *Job Hunter's Handbook,* page 240.
5. Charles Swindoll, *Living Above the Level of Mediocrity* (Waco, TX: Word Books, 1987), page 98.

Chapter Nine: R.S.V.P.
1. *Sunshine Magazine,* as quoted in *The Speaker's Sourcebook,* page 180.
2. Alan Bloom, as quoted in *Time,* October 17, 1988, pages 74-77.
3. Henry Wadsworth Longfellow, "A Psalm of Life," in *The Family Album of Favorite Poems,* ed. P. Edward Ernest (New York: G. P. Putnam's Sons, 1959), page 32.

BIBLIOGRAPHY

I recommend the following resources, many of which have influenced my own research and thought, for further reading in the area of vocational planning.

Allen, Ronald B. *The Majesty of Man.* Portland, OR: Multnomah Press, 1984.

Bolles, Richard N. *The Three Boxes of Life.* Berkeley, CA: Ten Speed Press, 1978.

Bolles, Richard N. *What Color Is Your Parachute?* Berkeley, CA: Ten Speed Press, 1990.

Drucker, Peter F. *The Effective Executive.* New York: Harper and Row, 1966.

Haldane, Bernard. *Career Satisfaction and Success.* Seattle, WA: AMACOM, 1988.

Herzberg, Frederick. *Work and the Nature of Man.* Cleveland,

OH: The World Publishing Company, 1966.

Holland, John. *Making Vocational Choices.* Englewood Cliffs, NJ: Prentice Hall, 1985.

Jaffe, Dennis T., and Cynthia D. Scott. *Take This Job and Love It.* New York: Simon and Schuster, 1988.

Laughlin, Rodney S. *The Job Hunter's Handbook: A Christian Guide.* Waco, TX: Word Books, 1985.

Miller, Arthur, and Ralph Mattson. *Finding a Job You Can Love.* Nashville, TN: Thomas Nelson Publishers, 1982.

Miller, Arthur, and Ralph Mattson. *The Truth About You.* Berkeley, CA: Ten Speed Press, 1977.

Myers, Isabel Briggs. *Gifts Differing.* Palo Alto, CA: Consulting Psychologists Press, 1980.

Parker, Yana. *The Damn Good Resume Guide.* Berkeley, CA: Ten Speed Press, 1983.

Peabody, Larry. *Secular Work Is Full-Time Service.* Fort Washington, PA: Christian Literature Crusade, 1973.

Sherman, Doug, and William Hendricks. *Your Work Matters to God.* Colorado Springs, CO: NavPress, 1988.

Staub, Dick, and Jeff Trautman. *Career Kit.* Seattle, WA: Intercristo, 1985.

Wilson, Earl D. *The Discovered Self.* Downers Grove, IL: Inter-Varsity Press, 1985.

Wilson, Earl D. *The Undivided Self.* Downers Grove, IL: Inter-Varsity Press, 1983.